# CHINA ONLINE

**The Author**
Véronique Michel is a true multilingual netizen.
She has spent 25 years abroad (notably in Japan
and China) and she obtained diplomas in Asian
and European languages. Véronique Michel is a
freelance translator and conference speaker on
multiculturalism. Please contact the author at
lachinebranchee@hotmail.fr for any comments.

# CHINA ONLINE

## NETSPEAK AND WORDPLAY USED BY OVER 700 MILLION CHINESE INTERNET USERS

VÉRONIQUE MICHEL

Illustrations by
Claude Müller, Sébastien Koval and Marcio Lobo

**TUTTLE** Publishing

Tokyo | Rutland, Vermont | Singapore

# Contents

4

**PART 2**
# WORD PLAY: HOW IT REVEALS TODAY'S CHINESE MIND

# Introduction

This book is a unique journey of discovery into the heart of contemporary China.

The first part sheds light on underground Chinese culture through a range of popular modern-day "tribes" that flourish on the Internet and reflect the diversification of Chinese society. The reader will discover the thousand-and-one ways leading to "Gross Domestic Happiness," as well as the secret of having a harmonious married life.

The second part focuses on the official "common language" (普通话 **pǔtōnghuà**) and the ingredients of Chinese humor that create a sense of connectedness among its speakers. We will decode the melodious phonetic puns, the magical spelling of characters, the ingenious numbers that "talk," and learn about the cultural intermingling of the Internet with the slang and catch phrases of over 700 million Chinese Web users . . . .

This first exploration has been compiled for the curious amateur, for students as well as experts, such as marketers and communications specialists seeking to understand a fast-evolving country.

# Pronunciation Guide

Below are a few elements of pronunciation in pinyin to help the reader. The example most used in schoolbooks is **ma**. The accent on the pinyin word indicates the pronunciation of the different tones.

| Character | Pinyin | Tone | Meaning |
|-----------|--------|------|---------|
| 妈 | **mā** | A high pitched, slightly elongated tone, which sounds like the "ahhh" a doctor might ask you to say. | mother |
| 麻 | **má** | A rising tone, from low to high, as though you were asking the question "What?" or "Why?" | hemp |
| 马 | **mǎ** | A falling and then rising tone, as if you were surprised at some announcement and asked, "Really?" | horse |
| 骂 | **mà** | A falling tone that drops sharply, as though you were telling someone to "Stop!" | to scold |

**PART 1**

# PORTRAITS

# China's Internet Boom

The economic development and reforms since the 1970s have transformed the face of China. There are no shortage of examples to illustrate these dramatic changes. At regional level, the considerable economic disparities have intensified the flow of "migrant workers" (民工 **míngōng**) from inland China to the coastal regions. The rise in living standards has led to the emergence of a middle class, which is now claiming its own identity. The government's one child policy has reshaped the family structure, now defined with the number "421" (4 grandparents, 2 parents and 1 child), since traditional filial piety has resulted in young people having to support as many as 6 elders. Nevertheless, according

to the new rule introduced in 2014 "if, in a couple, either parent is an only child, they are now eligible to have two children of their own."

In this period of social transition, the Internet has triggered a multitude of neologisms to depict contemporary society. The creations of fertile imaginations, some terms are invented from nothing, while others are borrowed from abroad. With humor and a hint of irony, netizens (Internet users) classify individuals sharing common traits as part of "tribes" or "clans" (族 **zú**). These include examples such as the "Mortgage Slaves," the "Ants" tribe, the "Moonlight" tribe .... The analogies are pertinent and people easily relate to them. Below the surface, these newly-created terms reveal trends that are shaking the foundations of Chinese society. The off-beat profiles that multiply on the Web show young people who are far more individualistic than their elders, women resisting pressures to marry, and young men free of convention. These virtual images echo a reality, which, while still marginal and essentially urban, is nevertheless very present.

# YOUNG PEOPLE IN
# CHINA TODAY

**W**hen a woman is pregnant in China she is said to "be happy" (有喜 **yǒuxǐ**): every year more than 15 million babies are born.

To ensure that their baby will be healthy and intelligent, women eat sea fish and walnuts during their pregnancy, the latter because they resemble a human brain. Whether from custom or superstition, parents try to time the year of the birth to coincide with an auspicious sign of the Chinese zodiac.

"Dragons" (龙 **lóng**) for instance, symbolize power, so the birth rate tends to increase in Dragon years.

In the same vein, a child's first name is a kind of premonition reflecting the parents' aspirations: grace, beauty, or elegance for girls; strength, perseverance, and success in the case of boys.

On the baby's first birthday celebration, it is customary to present the child with a variety of objects for it to "seize" (抓住 **zhuāzhù**) to identify its tastes and future potential. These may include a laptop, a violin, a book, or a banknote, in the hope of

divining that the child may one day become a computer engineer, a musician, a successful writer, or a businessperson.

In playschool the child will start learning several disciplines such as music, painting, singing, foreign languages, and dancing. The aim is to discover and nurture the child's potential as early as possible in a highly competitive environment.

School is mandatory and free for the first nine years, but any additional expenses (such as books and uniforms) are paid for by the parents. If they have the means, it is advised to give a financial contribution to the school.

In primary school, the little cherub will learn Chinese characters and copy them out assiduously. The verb "to copy"

in Chinese language also means "to learn" (学 **xué**). By extension "copying" one's teacher is a way of showing respect.

Discipline is the norm. Pupils rise when adults enter the room. They are divided into small groups and take it in turns to clean the classroom. They raise the flag every Monday and practice gymnastics in the morning. Every year on September 10, they celebrate Teachers' Day to express their gratitude.

Just like the Western adage "promoting a healthy mind in a healthy body," the good student must achieve the "Three Perfections" known as 3H, or the 三好 **sānhǎo** (the H for 好 **hǎo** meaning "good"). These stand for perfect "morality" (品德 **pǐndé**), good "results" (成绩 **chéngjì**), and good at "sports" (体育 **tǐyù**). Teachers and pupils use those criteria to select the "best in class." It is also well-regarded to take part in extracurricular activities, since it demonstrates the ability to socialize.

During their schooling, the children will learn the importance of improving themselves and contributing to harmony in their family, as well as supporting the country's prosperity, while observing a moderate attitude in all things. School is also the starting point for a real examination obstacle race.

In high school, cohorts of students (nearly 10 million each year) compete for university entrance every June. For three days their parents pamper their offspring and dose them with heavily advertised "miracle" potions. Drivers are forbidden to sound their horns in the vicinity of the exam centers and construction work is put on hold. The entire country holds its breath!

Once at university, young people are encouraged to become involved in projects to develop the countryside, such as "a student in every village." They are hired as civil servants or teachers for a set period of time, and in exchange obtain the sought-after urban "resident's permit" (户口 **hùkǒu**), authorizing them to settle in the city.

Students may not marry while at university, but must focus on exams and diplomas. To counter this, students launched the "Singles Day," held every year on November 11.

Their parents may help them in their search for a kindred spirit by meeting in parks to exchange photos of their children. When the young people finally find their partner of choice they may express their attachment by wearing amusing "partner clothing."

Millions of parents nurture similar dreams for their children, namely that they will enjoy a sparkling career. That means that

An example of partner clothing

after studying hard and graduating with a good degree, they will be hired by a major corporation and rise to dragon status—hence the expression "to become a dragon" (望子成龙 **wàng zǐ chéng lóng**); or, in the case of their daughters, "a phoenix" (望女成凤 **wàng nǚ chéng fèng**).

However, with the economic crisis and the rise in the number of graduates, the expression "exams decide the future" no longer fully applies. Even with degrees in their pockets, young people don't always find jobs or succeed in society. Many go abroad to complete their training and improve their chances. Despite the widespread belief that education equals upward social mobility, the path to success may take many detours, far from the traditional road to success . . . .

# Modern-day Tribes

## ■ The "Café Latte" Tribe
LATTE 族 **Latte zú**/拿铁族 **nátiě zú**

This refers to the Italian beverage *latte*, since the pronunciation resembles the English "late"—which may explain why the "Café Lattes" consider that haste makes waste.

They are indifferent to admiration from their peers and keep away from fast-food thinking. In fact, they are circumspect about the rush to earn money and the latest fads. In an evolving world, the "Café Lattes" strike a subtle balance between traditional and modern values. They do not hesitate to challenge preconceived ideas to establish new points of reference. Members of this tribe consider that you do not become an adult by putting a wedding ring on your finger, but only once you stand on your own two feet.

Hard workers but deep-down hedonists, the "Café Lattes" are

convinced that "a plant may produce new flowers, but we only have one youth" (花有重开日、人无再少年。 **huā yǒu chóngkāirì, rén wú zài shàonián**).

They therefore do not "take the branch for the root" (本末倒置 **běn mò dào zhì**)—that is to say, they do not put the cart before the horse. They will marry and have children, but only when they are financially secure.

## ■ The "Moonlight" or "Starlight" Tribe
月光族 **yuèguāng zú**/星光族 **xīngguāng zú**

The "Moonlight" tribe enjoys nothing more than throwing money down the drain.

The neologism stems from a contraction of "spending everything" (花光 **huāguāng**) and "monthly salary" (月薪 **yuèxīn**), which gives rise to "moonlight" (月光 **yuèguāng**). Similarly, by adding the Chinese character for "salary" (薪 **xīn**) to "finished" or "used up" (光 **guāng**), we create the poetic "starlight" (星光 **xīngguāng**).

The "Moonlight" tribe's extravagance is in great contrast with the frugality of previous generations. These "young people" (年轻人 **niánqīng rén**) like to splash their cash, and money burns a hole in their pockets. Consequently they are "broke at the end of the year" (年清人 **niánqīng rén**).

Curious and optimistic by nature, members of this tribe are fond of crazes and can easily become "credit card slaves" (卡奴 **kǎ nú**). A misquote from Shakespeare has been specially created for them: "to buy or not to buy, that is the question."

The best friends of monetary circulation, they often experience budgetary slippages. The "Moonlight" tribe sweeps aside the golden rule of austerity, persuaded that consumption is the supreme will of the people. Lenders of the last resort, they will even get into debt to please their friends and they personify the truism that "when you love, you do not count the cost."

At the other end of the spectrum from the "Moonlight" tribe is the "Tight-fisted" tribe (抠抠族 **kōukōu zú**), whose slogan could be "To save is glorious, to waste is scandalous." The "Ultra-thrifty" appreciate a quality and elegant lifestyle at an affordable price. They tend to go for bulk purchasing and coupons. However, they should not be confused with the "Stingy" tribe (酷抠族 **kùkōu zú**), who leads an austere lifestyle despite their comfortable incomes.

> 挣钱是一种能力，花钱是一种技术，
> 我能力有限，技术却很高。
> **zhèng qián shì yī zhǒng nénglì, huāqián shì yī**
> **zhǒng jìshù, wǒ nénglì yǒu xiàn, jìshù què hěn gāo.**
> Earning money requires ability; spending money
> requires a technique. My ability is limited,
> my technique is excellent.

# ■ The "Rush-Rush" Tribe
### 奔奔族 bēnbēn zú

Originally, this colloquial expression derives from the idiom "running east and walking west" (东奔西走 **dōngbēn xīzǒu**), which depicts a highly active person that bustles about but who does not confuse speed with haste. The members of the "Rush-Rush" tribe are intuitive, but they keep both feet on the ground. The Chinese character 奔 **bēn** stands for: "Running" (奔跑 **bēnpǎo**) and being "busy around" (奔波 **bēnbō**), "bubbling with a lot of energy" (热情奔放 **rèqíng bēnfàng**).

The "Rush-Rusher" has adopted the motto of the People's Republic of China regarding "self-reliance" (自力更生 **zìlìgèngshēng**). Caught in the maelstrom of change, he seeks to forge a glorious future for himself, thinking that, "if you do not work ardently when you are young, you will regret it when you are old" (少壮不努力，老大徒伤悲。**shàozhuàng bù nǔlì, lǎodà tú shāngbēi**). His unbending results-oriented philosophy serves as a compass for finding the right track.

The "Rush-Rusher" never stops nurturing his career, his good health, and his future, convinced by Confucius's advice that "at thirty one must stand firm" (三十而立 **sān shí ér lì**)—in other words, one has to be settled in life. Since his frenzy is time-consuming, this early riser is active 25 hours a day in the firm belief that more work means more money.

If you ask "Rush-Rushers" if they are busy, they may reply with a single name from Western antiquity: "Alexander!" (亚历

正能量！
**zhèng néng liàng!**
Positive energy!

Chinese Internet users have turned the advertising slogan "Just do it!" into "Just 加 jiā it" ("pile on the overtime").

山大！ **yàlìshāndà!**). In an amusing play on words, the phonetic transcription of "Alexander" has been kept but its spelling has been shifted to mean "under as much pressure as a mountain" (压力山大 **yālìshāndà**), which means "very stressed."

压力山大！
**yālìshāndà!**
I am very stressed!

The "Rush Rush" tribe is on the run at the "three time highs" (三高时代 **sān gāo shí dài**):

- Expensive house prices (房价高 **fángjià gāo**)
- Expensive car prices (车价高 **chējià gāo**)
- Expensive medical treatments (医疗高 **yīliáo gāo**)

"Rush-Rushers" excel at the art of remaining employable. They fine-tune their image and expand their networks through an active social life. In their eyes, fame and success are the best expressions of filial piety.

These busy bees are outstanding managers and know how to keep their wits about them. They are well-versed in risk assessment and always find a way for improving the yields of their share portfolios. Whatever situation they face, the "Rush-Rushers" will always bounce back after a blow. After all, doesn't "talent" (才 **cái**) rhyme with "fortune" (财 **cái**)? For them, the "Chinese dream" (中国梦 **zhōngguó mèng**) can be summarized by the "3 thoughts" (三想 **sān xiǎng**):

- To become rich (想暴富 **xiǎng bàofù**)
- To become famous (想成名 **xiǎng chéngmíng**)
- To live in a house (想住房 **xiǎng zhùfáng**)

## ■ The "Mortgage Slaves"
房奴 **fáng nú**

A TV series called *Dwelling Narrowness* (蜗居 **wōjū**) has been hotly debated across China. At a time of soaring house prices, it depicts, partly with realism, partly with parody, the obstacle race of white-collar workers fighting to become home owners.

The story is about the ups and downs in the lives of two sisters. In one episode, one of them says, "Every day when I wake up I see a list of our daily expenses that are linked to our mortgage, food, clothing, entertainment, transport, and home maintenance. They all relate to our urban lifestyle. They oblige us to pursue our efforts day after day."

The series gave rise to a "Snail Dwelling" tribe (蜗居族 **wōjū**

**zú**) and a cult expression, "My debts of gratitude have been repaid with my body" (人情债，我肉偿了。**rénqíngzhài, wǒ ròu cháng le**). In the story, one of the sisters has an affair with a pen-pushing bureaucrat who has the power to help her achieve the family dream of buying a home.

Like these heroines, many Chinese consider home ownership to be a precondition to family happiness. Someone who is a slave to his/her home is perceived as having a difficult life; but the alternative is worse and marginalizes people. With the rising cost of living, the situation has grown even harder and one of the most-used terms in China these past years was "rise" (涨 **zhǎng**) with reference to prices—hence the popular expression, "It's easy to be 'born' (生 **shēng**), easy to 'live' (活 **huó**) but complicated to earn a 'living' (生活 **shēnghuó**)."

In the same vein, the "Sunflower" tribe (葵花族 **kuíhuā zú**), who sees the sunny side of life, grew out of a reaction against this competitive environment, just like the "Zero Pascal" tribe (零帕族 **língpà zú**), named after Blaise Pascal, the mathematician who defined atmospheric pressure, but which has come to signify stress for netizens. Members of that tribe do not want to be swallowed by an escalating spiral of debts and loans. They simply aspire to be happy, free from obligations and financial harassment.

听说房价要下跌了。
**tīng shuō fáng jià yào xiàdiē le.**
I have heard that the price
of flats will fall.

喜大普本！
**xǐdàpǔbēn!**
What a wonderful piece of news!

| 喜大普奔 | | | |
|---|---|---|---|
| **xǐdàpǔbēn** | | | |
| What a wonderful piece of news | | | |
| These 4 Chinese characters are the abbreviation of 4 Chinese idiomatic expressions: | | | |
| 喜 | 大 | 普 | 奔 |
| **喜**闻乐见 **Xǐwénlèjiàn** Delighted to see and hear | **大**快人心 **DÀkuàirénxīn** Everybody is happy | **普**天同庆 **PǓtiāntóngqÌng** The whole world joins in the jubilation | **奔**走相告 **BĒNzǒuxiānggào** The piece of news spreads around |

## ■ The "Returnees from Overseas" (also called the "Overseas Returnees")
### 海归 **hǎiguī**

In the land of Confucius, education has always been perceived as the imperial road to guarantee upward social mobility.

The "multi-certificate holders" (本本族 **běnběn zú**) and other "certificate maniacs" (哈证族 **hāzhèng zú**) are legion. Because of the economic context, these clans now also include employees taking their skills "back to the furnace" (回炉 **huílú**) by signing up for evening classes to brush up their skills and broaden their job prospects.

Since it is preferable to have more than one string to one's bow, many young people go abroad to complete their education. They consider that "studying is like swimming against the tide" and "if you do not advance, you fall back" (学如逆水行舟，不进则退。 **xué rú nì shuǐ xíngzhōu, bújìn zé tuì**).

On their return to China they are "returnees from overseas" (海归 **hǎiguī**) and therefore referred to as "Sea Turtles" (海龟 **hǎiguī**), which is pronounced exactly the same way. If the job hunt of the "Sea Turtles" is fruitless, they join the ranks of people "waiting at home for a job" (海待 **hǎidài**), and are called "seaweed" (海带 **hǎidài**).

Among those staying at home, new categories have emerged in recent years:

- The group of young people who never leave home and "eat away" at their parents is called the "Bite-the-old" tribe (啃老族 **kěnlǎo zú**).  In the old days parents used to "keep one child for one's old age" (养儿防老 **yǎng ér fáng lǎo**). Today, couples take care of their elders so that they financially support their grandchildren (养老防儿 **yǎng lǎo fáng ér**).

- The "Rice-bowl test-taking" tribe (考碗族 **kǎowǎn zú**) is made up of the young people preparing for civil service entrance exams in search of an "iron rice bowl" (铁饭碗 **tiěfàn wǎn**)—that is to say, a safe, permanent job.

NOTE: Please be aware that 本本族 **běn běn zú** has three meanings: at the very beginning it meant "careless driver;" later on it meant "laptop holder;" and later still, "multi-certificate holder."

## ■ The "Low Carbon Footprint" Tribe
低碳一族 **dītàn yīzú**

This tribe strives to reduce its energy consumption and cut carbon emissions. Its name stems from a local government initiative in Chongqing, a megalopolis of more than 32 million inhabitants. The members of this tribe aim at raising awareness of the air pollution which they call "airpocalypse," literally "Judgment Day atmosphere" (末日空气 **mòrì kōngqì**), and "the fog and haze" (雾霾 **wùmái**) which sometimes envelops large cities.

A rapid economic growth has led to major ecological damage in the workshop of the world. In the face of global climate changes, many local initiatives have sprung up to lay down the foundations of "a better life in a better city" as Shanghai Universal Expo slogan put it for a prosperous and sustainable development promoting renewable energies.

At grass roots level, advocates of a BIOTIFUL planet help raise ecological awareness. They encourage an eco-chic lifestyle and promote a "green civilization." They also fight to eradicate the "Unidentified Fat-food Objects (UFO's)" and all types of junk food that have invaded our plates. The "Low Carbon Footprint" tribe is in line with the Chinese tradition by which "When the desires of man and heaven are in agreement, harmony reigns between man and nature."

> 你浪费的粮食都会堵在你去往天堂的路上。
> **nǐ làngfèi de liángshí dōu huì dǔ zài
> nǐ qù wǎng tiāntáng de lùshàng.**
> All the wasted food you left will block your road to Heaven.

# ■ The "Ants" Tribe
### 蚁族 yǐ zú

The young people in this tribe share three characteristics with that industrious insect: they are intelligent, they look weak yet they are strong, and they gather together.

The "Ants" make their first steps at university or technical institutes, where they acquire precious skills. With their diploma in their pocket, the "Ants" leave their family cocoon to catch the train of economic growth. They expect a return on their investment: finding a job and building their nest.

Despite their qualifications, they may not meet those hoped-for professional opportunities and they experience fluctuating fortune in an erratic job market.

In insecure jobs and deprived of social security, they end up living at the outskirts of small or large cities, where they form close-knit communities.

> 我们要考虑你的 "前途"。
> **wǒmen yào kǎolǜ nǐ de "qiántú".**
> We want to consider your prospects.

> 前途还是 "钱途"？
> **qiántú háishi "qiántú"?**
> My "prospects" or my "wage increase"?

The "Ants'" initial euphoria may therefore give way to disillusionment, but their willpower wins over uncertainty and carries the day. With their quiet strength, they know they will ultimately triumph over obstacles on the road to success. After all, are they not the architects of the Chinese dream?

Their slogan could be "Let dreams fly!" (让梦想飞 **ràng mèng-xiǎng fēi**). Or, more pragmatically, "Let wages fly!" (让工资飞! **ràng gōngzī fēi!**), an expression derived from the popular film *Let the Bullets Fly!* (让子弹飞! **ràng zǐdàn fēi!**).

让工资飞!
**ràng gōngzī fēi!**
Let wages fly!

## ■ The "Strawberry" Tribe
草莓族 **cǎoméi zú**

This name originates from Taiwan. In a cutting-edge competitive world, the "Strawberry" tribe strives toward personal fulfillment. It is made up of young people who are still inexperienced in the job market and hostile to any kind of pressure. They are not afraid of work, but because stress is definitely not their cup of tea, these trendy youngsters have been compared to strawberries. They are beautiful and yet fragile, and require optimal climatic conditions to grow to their fullest potential. Their motto could be "work to live," rather than "live to work." Deepdown, "Strawberries" are convinced hedonists aspiring to make the most of life.

It is said that companies are composed of an exotic cocktail of employees. The most fragile ones are nicknamed the "Puddings" tribe (布丁族 **bùdīng zú**), or the "Tofu" tribe (豆腐族 **dòufu zú**), while their direct opposites are called the "Coconuts" tribe (椰子族 **yēzi zú**), as they are protected by a strong shell. You might also encounter some members of the "Durian" tribe (榴莲族 **liúlián zú**), named after a pungent Southeast Asian fruit. Its members are subject to numerous constraints and are rather short-tempered.

> 不怕事多，就怕多事。
> **bú pà shì duō, jiù pà duō shì.**
> I am not afraid of a lot of work,
> I am only afraid of trouble.

## ■ The "Corporate Insects"
公司蛀虫 gōngsī zhùchóng

This is another play on words based on the homophones for the "moth" (驻虫 zhùchóng) and "the one who takes roots" (蛀虫 zhùchóng). Even though they enjoy excellent working conditions and a high salary, the "Corporate Insects" are city-

dwellers who feel melancholic, as they are far away from their native province. At the end of the working day, the "Corporate Insects" feel blue. They have no welcoming place to go to socialize and they are reluctant to return home. As a result, these workaholics put in extra overtime or linger at their desks to surf the Web. Being cut off from the outside world, they get attached to the companies they work for: it is the place where they find their soulmates and their friends. Imperceptibly, their professional life consumes their private life.

In China, people are always being told that chicken soup helps to dissipate loneliness. This is encapsulated in the notorious expression, "What I am eating is not noodles, it is loneliness,"

and leads to endless variations on that theme: "What I am smoking is not a cigarette, it is solitude," or "What I am writing is not a book, it is sorrow." In other words, "I am not alone, loneliness is accompanying me" (哥，不寂寞。因为有寂寞陪着哥。**gē, bú jìmò. yīnwéi yǒu jìmò péizhe gē**).

哥喝的不是汤，是寂寞。
**gē hē de búshì tāng, shì jìmò.**
What I am drinking is not soup, it is loneliness.

Chicken soup dissipates loneliness.

## ■ The "Crazy Jargon" Tribe
怪字族 **guàizì zú**

This tribe is made up of all those people who invent their own language on the Internet. In China there are more than 500 million smartphone users, more than 700 million active users of social networks and one billion posts published daily on the

Internet. The average age of Chinese Internet users is between 20 and 35, and they live mainly in the cities. The most used search engines are sina.com, baidu.com ("100 degrees"), and sohu.com ("the fox"), while the most popular messaging site is QQ.com—which, to the Chinese, sounds just like the English word "cute." Chinese netizens "rummage through Ali Baba's cave" on alibaba.com or "hunt for treasures" on taobao.com. They can explore the "four corners of the earth" on tianya.com, seek "happiness" on kaixino01.com, and communicate with "everyone" on renren.com, a large social networking site.

Since the advent of the Internet, plenty of amusing digital jargon has flourished. Turning their nose up at conventional language usage, Internet geeks manipulate with virtuosity the homophones that abound in their mother tongue. They borrow foreign words and grammatical usage (mostly from English, Japanese, and Korean), and throw overboard rules and syntax, since creativity is a must. Characters are interwoven or deconstructed, and drawings proliferate.

Sheltered from the eyes of adults (and any other unwelcome visitors), young people employ these stylized languages to communicate among themselves. Their jargon is a source of conflict between them and anxious parents, who can make neither head nor tail of it and sound the alarm. Meanwhile, baffled experts conduct research to try to decipher this new type of prose.

The most famous language originated from Taiwan and is known as the "Martian language" (火星文 **huǒxīng wén**). It originally came from a movie entitled *Shaolin Soccer,* directed by Stephen Chow, in which one character declares that "The Earth is too dangerous, let's return to Mars!" The Martian style has been emulated by many and was more than just a jargon restricted to the happy few. It left the realm of the virtual to represent a laidback style, where a cool attitude is distinguished by its "China touch."

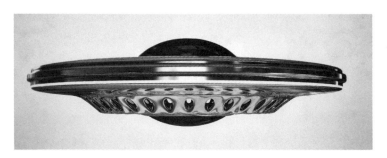

It has opened the way for other innovative languages, such as the "Roaring style" (咆哮体 **páoxiàotǐ**). This style makes use of a great deal of exclamation marks and expressions, such as 伤不起 **shāngbùqǐ**, which indicates that the threshold of tolerance has been reached and the situation has become unbearable.

Let's find out more by examining some examples.

# ORZ

ORZ is a well-known image signifying respect and humility. It symbolizes somebody bowing down.

## Chinese characters

Some obsolete characters are being revived:

The character 囧 **jiǒng** used to describe "astonishment" or "sadness." If you give free rein to your imagination, you may customize it at will to convey all kinds of messages to reflect your state of mind.

囧 **Jiǒng** has become famous through the popular comedy movie, *Lost on Journey* (人在囧途 **rén zài jiǒng tú**).

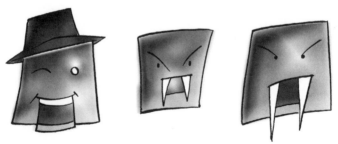

囧 **Jiǒng** can be adapted as an emoticon to fit any situation!

# 槑

The character 槑 **méi** originally means "plum" but in Internet speak it has come to indicate "boredom multiplied by two" or "stupidity" (呆 **dāi**). The character can also mean "insipid" or "dull-witted," but it can be adapted (see character, right).

槑 **méi** can also be the start of a romance.

In a connected world, hybrid expressions have emerged, the most notorious being "hen geili" (很给力 **hěn gěilì**), which means "awesome" or "cool." It was coined by Chinese netizens who then developed an English variation, "gelivable," which has spread over the Internet and has even been adopted as far away as France.

很给力！
**hěn gěilì!**
Gelivable!

酷 **kù** on a jacket means "cool"!

# ■ The "Luxury" Tribe
## 辣奢族 làshē zú

辣奢 **làshē** derives from the English word "luxury." This tribe is composed of individuals who cannot resist the temptation of designer labels and are ready to sacrifice the essential to acquire the superfluous. Their maxim is:

"The shirt makes the man and the saddle makes the horse" (人靠衣服马靠鞍 **rén kào yīfu mǎ kào ān**).

China has become the new Eldorado for luxury brands, with typical buyers aged under 30. In their quest for "the best of the best," the "Luxury" tribe embarks on a luxury mania hunt. What matters for them is to "stand out from others" (与众不同 **yǔ zhòng bùtóng**) but always with a taste for elegance.

While luxury was condemned in the past, it is now the mark of success, and brand prestige reflects on the individual and his/her social status.

The *People's Daily* once published a survey about the aspirations of the average man in the street. They included "getting rich, traveling around the world, making China the most powerful country in the world, having a villa and a luxury car."

# ■ The "Otaku" Tribe
### 御宅族 yùzhái zú

This tribe's name also comes from Japan, where *otaku* originally meant "at home."

The "Otaku" tribe comprises people who stay cooped up at home. With a simple click of the mouse, these geeks escape with enthusiasm to the fairytale world of Internet and video games.

In a country where sociability and competitiveness are key values, people are disconcerted by the voluntary isolation of this tribe. Studies show that about 24 million Internet "addicts" are lost in the Chinese virtual labyrinth, causing parents to seek council from specialists or institutions that sometimes resort to radical disciplinary approaches.

In China, 宅 **zhái** is the popular expression for "staying at

By phonetic coincidence, the characters used in the Chinese name for "Marie Curie" literally mean "the woman who stays at home" (居里夫人 **jūlǐ fūrén**). Her male counterpart is "Picasso" 毕加索 (**bìjiāsuǒ**), a name that has been shifted to describe the geek who is "chained to his home" (闭家锁 **bìjiāsuǒ**).

41

home," while in Japan *otaku* has acquired a second life with a different meaning, since it now applies to *aficionados*—that is, individuals who are totally devoted to a pastime and have developed a real expertise in the field. In other words, it no longer points to an addiction, but to a passion.

When they do manage to detach themselves from the Net: it has been known for "Otaku" to resort to *seppuku* (ritual suicide) to disappear from social networks . . . .

---

## ■ The "Couch Potato" Tribe
沙发土豆族 **shāfā tǔdòu zú**

This is a literal translation of the English term. It designates people who spend their evenings, if not their days, lounging on the sofa with a remote control fossilized in their hands. This stress relief method appears to be used across all social categories around the world. For the "potatoes," "Every bird likes its own nest the best" (金窝银窝不如自己的草窝。**jīnwō yínwō bùrú zìjǐ de cǎowō**).

你幸福吗?
**Nǐ xìngfú ma?**
Are you happy?

## ■ The "Thumb" Tribe
拇指族 **mǔzhǐ zú**

This neologism comes from Japan, where it is called *Oyayu-bizoku*. It refers to technophile texting virtuosos, whatever the mobile device. China has the largest number of smartphone users in the world and the Chinese have created all kinds of abbreviations when emailing or texting. This tribe is also called "the lower one's head" tribe (低头族 **dītóu zú**), or "the fingertips" clan (指尖族 **zhǐjiān zú**). Its members enjoy nothing more than playing with their "mobile phone" (手机 **shǒujī**) which they often call the "machine in their claws" (爪机 **zhuǎ jī**).

## 1. Abbreviations borrowed from English

| Abbreviation | English |
|---|---|
| BF | Boyfriend |
| BTW | By the way |
| FFE | Friends forever |
| GF | Girlfriend |

| Abbreviation | English |
|---|---|
| IC | I see |
| IMHO | In my humble opinion |
| MSULKeCraZ | Miss you like crazy |
| OF COZ | Of course |
| RUOK | Are you OK? |
| ROFL | Rolling on the floor laughing |
| TTUL | Talk to you later |

## 2. Romanized abbreviations from Chinese

| Abbreviation | Term | Explanation |
|---|---|---|
| BB | 拜拜 **bàibài**<br>宝贝 **bǎobèi** | Either goodbye or treasure/darling |
| BC | 白痴 **báichī** | Idiot |
| BCM | 别臭美 **bié chòuměi** | Stop showing off! |
| BH | 彪悍 **biāohàn** | Intrepid/valiant |
| BT | 变态 **biàntài** | Abnormal/bizarre |
| FB | 腐败 **fǔbài** | Originally meant "corruption," but now used to mean "squander money on living it up" |
| FS | 发牢骚 **fā láosāo** | To grumble/complain |
| GX | 恭喜 **gōngxǐ** | Congratulations |
| JS | 奸商 **jiānshāng** | Dubious storekeeper (who sells counterfeit goods) |
| LD | 领导 **lǐngdǎo** | Either boss, wife, or girlfriend |
| LG | 老公 **lǎogōng** | husband |

| Abbreviation | Term | Explanation |
|---|---|---|
| LM | 靓妹 liàngmèi | A beautiful girl |
| LP | 老婆 lǎopó | Wife |
| LR | 懒人 lǎnrén | Lazybones |
| MF | 麻烦 máfan | Troublesome/irritating |
| MS | 马上 mǎshàng | Immediately |
| | 貌似 màosì | To pretend/put on airs |
| OU | 偶 ǒu (used on the Internet instead of 我 wǒ) | I/me |
| PF | 佩服 pèifú | Well done! |
| PMP | 拍马屁 pāi mǎpì | Boot licker |
| PLMM | 漂亮美眉 piàoliàng měiméi | A beautiful woman |
| SG | 帅哥 shuàigē | A handsome guy |
| +U | 加油 jiāyóu | Keep it up/Go on! |
| WUWU | 呜呜 wūwū | Sad (to find regrettable) |
| WL | 网恋 wǎngliàn | A virtual romance |
| YBBL | 一般般了 yì bānbān le | So-so/not brilliant |
| XIXIHAHA | 嘻嘻哈哈 xīxīhāhā | Laughter |

## 3. Abbreviations using numbers

| Abbreviation | Term | Explanation |
|---|---|---|
| 3X | 3谢 sān xiè | Thanks |
| 8K7 | 不客气 búkèqi | You are welcome! |

45

# ■ The "Flea" Tribe
## 跳蚤族 tiàozǎo zú

"Fleas" start looking for work as soon as they graduate. They will grab the first job that comes their way and then take their time prospecting for a better one. This attitude has given rise to the expression "ride a donkey while looking for a horse" (骑驴找马 qí lǘ zhǎo mǎ). The donkey symbolizes a routine job with no prospects, while the horse represents a good opportunity.

"Fleas" are curious and do not like to be tied down. They enjoy life's pleasures and know that there is no cure for regret. The "Fleas" see themselves as "pearls of the ocean" (沧海遗珠 cānghǎi yí zhū) and consider that their talents are not always appreciated and rewarded at their full worth. They may not have a career strategy, but they strike at the right moment.

The homophonic pun for "the flea that jumps out of joy" (高兴跳蚤 gāoxìng tiàozǎo) is "the flea that jumps on a high salary" (高薪跳蚤 gāoxīn tiàozǎo), which clearly reveals the "Flea's" intention. All in all, the "Flea" always places the bar higher.

## ■ The "Pressure Cooker" Tribe
高压锅族 **gáoyāguō zú**

This neologism emerged after a 2012 survey by journalists, which showed that 45 percent of respondents believed themselves to be stressed, 25 percent considered themselves to be very stressed, and 3 percent at the end of their tether.

> 最近工作压力很大，元芳，你怎么看？
> **zuìjìn gōngzuò yālì hěn dà, Yuánfāng, nǐ zěnme kàn?**
> We've been working under a lot of pressure recently, Yuanfang, what do you think about it?

Members of the "Pressure Cooker" tribe work like crazy because they know very well that nothing will be handed to them on a plate. They are caught between family and professional obligations and susceptible to stress, or at the very least, a great deal of tension. With no reliable social security coverage or pension, these young people have to take care of their elderly parents while saving up for their children's future. They consider that no work means no future, but also that no home means no wife, and no status means no social recognition. Members of the "Pressure Cooker" tribe have a heavy burden to bear and a "long road to travel" (任重道远 **rènzhòng dàoyuǎn**).

Despite their desire to conform, they have a limited capacity for resistance and may find themselves on the verge of a nervous breakdown. Faced with this "dog's life" (生活不如意 **shēnghuó bù rúyì**), they need to stand back and let go. Their health and happiness depend on it.

# ■ The *Tuhao* or the "No Class *Nouveaux Riches*" (also called the tasteless *nouveaux riches*)
## 土豪 **tǔháo**

土豪 **tǔháo** is composed of 土 **tǔ** (land) and 豪 **háo** (powerful). A long time ago 土豪 **tǔháo** indicated rich and tyrannic landlords.

Nowadays 土豪 **tǔháo** may be used to refer to "no class *nouveaux riches*," that is to say "people with money but without style": 土 **tǔ** refers to "lack of taste" and 豪 **háo** refers to "rich and powerful." Hence, 土豪 **tǔháo** means "to be a tasteless rich person" (很土的富豪 **hěn tǔ de fùháo**). Some members of this tribe like to "show off" on the Internet "their salary," "their racing cars" or "their homes" (晒工资，晒自己的跑车，晒自己的房间 **shài gōngzī, shài zìjǐ de pǎochē, shài zìjǐ de fángjiān**).

> 有钱有酒，必有朋友。
> **yǒu qián yǒu jiǔ, bì yǒu péngyǒu.**
> If you have money and free drinks, you will have friends.

Since the "No Class *Nouveaux Riches*" particularly like the new iPhone 5s, the word 土豪 **tǔháo** also symbolizes social status. "Local gold tyrant" (土豪金 **tǔháo jīn**) is the name for the Gold iPhone 5s launched in China in 2013 by Apple. In Chinese culture, gold represents wealth.

> 土豪，
> 我们做朋友吧!
> **tǔháo, wǒmen zuò péngyǒu ba!**
> Tuhao, let's become friends!

The cat is "acting cute" (卖萌 **màimeng**), a very popular attitude on the Chinese Internet.

MEN

# THE "FOUR GENTLEMEN" AND MODERN-DAY MEN

The "Four Gentlemen" (四君子 **sì jūnzǐ**) refer to the four plants that illustrate perfection. Far from being a thing of the past, their characteristics symbolize an honest gentleman, and by extension, the perfect man.

 The "plum" (梅 **méi**) stands for pride. It is as persevering as it is tenacious, and despite the cold, it blossoms in the dead of winter to display all its glory.

 The "orchid" (兰 **lán**) incarnates modesty. Its talents are concealed behind its delicate fragrance. To fully appreciate the man it represents, one needs to use one's heart.

 The "bamboo" (竹 **zhú**) symbolizes someone who is upright and flexible. It grows throughout the year, never fading, and has come to represent eternal youth.

 The "chrysanthemum" (菊 **jú**) stands for purity. It flourishes and displays its beauty, even in the most inhospitable places.

## A survey of Chinese men

Chinese men are usually portrayed as ambitious, attached to male friendship and with a strong tendency to control their emotions. When they marry, they become the head of the family and take on numerous responsibilities.

In his renowned *Chinese Man Investigation*, Zhang Jie Hai drew up a list of their strengths and weaknesses. Here is a brief summary:

| Rank | Merits | Rank | Shortcomings |
|---|---|---|---|
| 1 | Responsible | 1 | Introverted |
| 2 | Serious | 2 | Macho |
| 3 | Hard-working | 3 | Miserly |
| 4 | Pragmatic | 4 | Egocentric |
| 5 | Attached to traditional values | 5 | Hesitant |
| 6 | Reserved | 6 | Placid |
| 7 | Attentive | 7 | Narrow-minded |

The sixth shortcoming is supposedly the antithesis of what many Chinese women believe to be a common quality in foreign men, who are regarded as dynamic, curious, romantic, sensual, and witty. True or not?

# Modern-day Tribes

## ■ The "Diamond Bachelor"
### 钻石王老五 zuànshí wánglǎowǔ

As heir to a wealthy family, the
"Diamond Bachelor" is not in the same
category as other common mortals.
He was born with a silver spoon in
his mouth and has a "triple A" rating.
Professional success and social status
are imperatives. He is always dressed to
the nines and his future is tailor-made.
Refinement is the *sine qua non* condition
to seducing him. Some "Diamond
Bachelors" may consider that "Life and
death rest in the hands of fate, rich and
noble are arranged by heaven" (生死
有命，富贵在天。 **shēngsǐ yǒu mìng,
fùguì zài tiān**).

Golf and luxury watches are
external signs of wealth.

After the wedding, he metamorpho-
ses into a "gold tortoise" (金龟婿 **jīnguīxù**), in other words, a
rich husband. The term comes from the Tang Dynasty (618–907),
when only the elite was allowed to wear bags with the tortoise
symbol on it.

At another stage, the "tortoise" may change into a "seagull"
(海鸥 **hǎi'ōu**), which stands for a "serial entrepreneur," constantly flying around the world for business.

Since humor is never far away, some women consider that
once married to a "Diamond Bachelor" they would be happy for
"the diamond to stay and the man to go!" (钻石留下，王老五可
以走了 **zuànshí liúxià, wánglǎowǔ kěyǐ zǒu le**).

## ■ The "Affordable" Man
经济适用男 **jīngjì shìyòng nán**

The expression derives from "affordable apartment" (经济适用房 **jīngjì shìyòng fáng**). The "Affordable" Man is both composed and straightforward. Despite his traditional mindset, he is not macho and is often regarded as a potential high net worth asset.

He may be quite ordinary in appearance, but Mr. Perfect is devoted to his wife. He hands over his entire salary and respects her choices. And the cherry on the cake is that while he may not be a master chef, he certainly can be useful in the kitchen! His favorite TV program is "the Chinese food culture is a bite of pleasure" (中国饮食文化就是舌尖上的快乐 **zhōngguó yǐnshí wénhuà jiù shì shéjiānshàng de kuàilè**).

> 我老婆是我的**总理**。
> **wǒ lǎopo shì wǒ de zǒnglǐ.**
> My wife is my prime minister.

> 明白了! 她**总**是有**理**。
> **míngbái le... tā zǒngshì yǒu lǐ!**
> I understand... she is always right!

## ■ The "Three Highs" Man
三高男 **sāngāo nán**

The "Three Highs" Man emerged during the Japanese economic boom years and refers to a man with three major assets:

- A higher education (高学历 **gāo xuélì**)
- Tall in height (高个子 **gāo gèzi**)
- A high income (高收入 **gāo shōurù**)

A "rocket manager" (火箭干部 **huǒjiàn gànbù**)
is a go-getter with a meteoric professional career.

A golden boy with a competitive nature, this type of man gets a rush of adrenalin from taking risks. A born leader, he does not go in for half measures and dislikes everyday routine. His trendy and elegant dress sense is one of his attractions.

His motto might be, "If you don't enter the tiger's lair, how will you capture the cubs?" (不入虎穴焉得虎子？ **bú rù hǔxué yāndé hǔzi?**)—in other words, nothing ventured, nothing gained.

Since humor is omnipresent in China, the three trump cards can easily be reinterpreted as:

- A high level of debt (高债务水平 **gāo zhàiwù shuǐpíng**)
- A high level of cholesterol (高血糖 **gāo xuètáng**)
- A high risk of a heart attack (心脏病发作的风险高 **xīnzàng-bìng fāzuò de fēngxiǎn gāo**)

---

## ■ The "Three Lows" Man
### 三低男 sāndī nán

女士优先
**nǚshì yōuxiān**
Ladies first

A "Three Lows" Man

Of a humble social background, these ordinary men have three modest, yet well-appreciated characteristics among women:

- Low profile (humility) (低姿态 **dī zītài**)
- Low risk (stable job) (低风险 **dī fēngxiǎn**)
- Low controls (not possessive about their wives) (低约束力 **dī yuēshùlì**)

These men are indifferent to artifacts and quite happy to stay out of the limelight. They project a reassuring image and are relaxed in appearance. Their dress code is practical rather than sophisticated and in their work lives they opt for stable jobs.

With humor, the three assets can be summed up as follows:

- Low degree of machismo (不太大男子主义 **bú tài dà nánzǐzhǔyì**)
- Low propensity for infidelity (比较忠实 **bǐjiào zhōngshí**)
- Low risk of jealousy (嫉妒心没有那么强 **jídùxīn méiyǒu nàme qiáng**)

## ■ The "Herbivore" Man (also called the "Herbivorous" Man)
草食男 **cǎoshí nán**

Several years ago, a well-known Japanese journalist, Maki Fukasawa, coined this term to describe a new type of man. "Herbivores" have thrown the "Carnivores'" values to the wind and "Carnivores" (i.e., the more enterprising and macho "gentleman swindler" types), now represent yesterday's man.

神马都是浮云。
**shénmǎ dōu shì fú yún.**
Everything's just a floating cloud.

This expression caused a buzz and means "nothing really matters."

"Herbivores" dream of making their lives a bed of roses and avoid rollercoaster emotions. In their eyes, men and women are equals and they often play the role of confidante for their female friends. They are certainly no lady killers. Any woman aspiring to seduce a "Herbivore" will have to break the ice and make the first move.

---

## ■ The "Phoenix" Man
凤凰男 **fènghuáng nán**

This neologism derives from a popular expression "a phoenix takes flight from the heart of the mountain" (山窝里飞出的金凤凰。**shānwō lǐ fēichū de jīn fènghuáng**). It refers to a man from a rural area that has succeeded professionally and now lives in the city. He is a self-made man, devoted to his family back home and supporting it financially.

The phoenix is the bird that rises from its ashes.

Is there such a thing as the attraction of opposites? There is a great deal of popular press coverage in China about the tumultuous relationships of female "Peacocks" from rich families with male "Phoenixes" of humble origin.

## ■ The "Diligent Bull" (also called the "Promising Bull")
牛奋男 niúfèn nán

The "Diligent Bull" is as solid as a rock. The trademarks of this tireless fighter are hard work and perseverance. He has a clear sense of responsibility and takes his commitments to heart. Neither macho nor arrogant, he is recognized as trustworthy and faithful.

The "Diligent Bull" has an insecure job and he is not rolling in money, but he will make strenuous efforts to consolidate his gains and improve the family's finances. In his mind, "patience is the mother of success" (耐心是成功之母 **nàixīn shì chénggōng zhī mǔ**).

Women see these pragmatic men as having a very positive aura. They consider them a safe haven and a good investment for the future. Are not care and consideration more valuable than the most luxurious gifts?

Many Chinese men meet their wives every evening
at the factories they work in, and give them
a ride home on their electric bikes.

## ■ The "Perfect" Man
### 高富帅 gāofùshuài

In 2012, a neologism was created to describe the "perfect" man (高富帅 **gāofùshuài**). It is composed of three characters meaning tall, rich, and handsome.

| 高富帅 gāofùshuài | | |
|---|---|---|
| Tall<br>高 **gāo** | Rich<br>富 **fù** | Handsome<br>帅 **shuài** |

This can be interpreted as ideals that any man can achieve through his own efforts:

- "High," or "tall," refers to a high intelligence quotient (高在智商 **gāo zài zhìshāng**)
- "Rich" refers to talents (富有才华 **fù yǒu cáihuá**)
- "Handsome" refers to deeds/action (帅于行动 **shuài yú xíngdòng**)

Netizens have devised an alternative amusing interpretation:

| 高 **gāo** | 富 **fù** is replaced by a homophone 负 **fù** | 帅 **shuài** is replaced by rash (马虎 **mǎhu**) and careless (草率 **cǎoshuài**) |
|---|---|---|
| **高**度近视<br>**GĀO**dù jìnshì<br>Very short-sighted | **负**债累累<br>**FÙ**zhài lěilěi<br>Over-indebted | 做事马虎草**率**<br>zuòshì mǎhu cǎo**SHUÀI**<br>Rash and careless in all that he does |

## ■ The "Poor" Man
屌丝 **diǎosī**

我不是富二代，我是负二贷。
**wǒ bú shì fù èr dài, wǒ shì fù èr dài.**
I'm not second generation rich,
I'm two-loan poor.

The "Poor" Man, sometimes called the "DIORS," has to fight to make his way in life. This neologism created a buzz and refers to young people from modest working class families, or young migrants.

Talking about his situation he would say:

每当我找到了成功的钥匙，
就有人把锁给换了。
**měi dāng wǒ zhǎo dào le chénggōng de yàoshí,**
**jiù yǒu rén bǎ suǒ gěi huàn le.**
Every day when I look for the key to success,
it appears that the lock has been changed.

WOMEN

# THE HISTORIC "FOUR BEAUTIES" AND MODERN-DAY WOMEN

n Chinese tradition the "four beauties" of antiquity (四大美女 **sì dà měinǚ**) symbolize women's attractiveness. They have well-known legends and histories.

- Xi Shi (sixth century BCE) became a spy for the Kingdom of Yue and brought about the downfall of Fuchai, the King of Wu.

- Wang Zhaojun (first century BCE) was forced to become a concubine of the King of the Xiongnu tribe to prevent war.

- Diaochan (second century AD) bewitched a despotic warlord and persuaded his most trusted general to murder him.

- Yang Guifei (eighth century AD) had a passionate affair with the Tang dynasty emperor Xuanzong. During a rebellion she was put to death in front of her lover, who later died of grief.

An expression was created for these four muses that is still in use today: Faced with such beauty, "fish forget to swim, wild geese stop beating their wings, the moon turns away, and flowers are put to shame" (沉鱼落雁，闭月羞花。**chényú luòyàn, bìyuè xiūhuā**).

The archetypal Chinese beauty of the past would have an oval face, symbolized by a watermelon seed, cheeks the color of a peach, and a mouth in the shape of a cherry. She would be as "slender as a willow" (杨柳细腰 **yángliǔxìyāo**) with skin as immaculate as a lotus root. In terms of ideal proportions, an idiomatic expression comparing the legendary thinness of the empress Zhao Feiyan with the generous curves of Yang Guifei, reminds us that "all women, whether slender or round, are beautiful and attractive" (环肥燕瘦 **huánféiyànshòu**).

A pale complexion is still a key criterion of beauty. The sun is therefore perceived as an enemy and anti-tanning treatments are popular. However, the "slim is beautiful" trend has also reached the country.

In terms of image and career, cosmetic surgery is considered an investment. Every year more than one million people in China go under the scalpel to lengthen their nose or legs, make their jaws more oval shaped, change their  eyelids to double eyelids, or make their lips thinner. For men and women alike, the body has become an asset to preserve and beauty is "constructed," with nothing left to chance.

# Modern-day Tribes

## ■ The "3 No's" Woman
三不女人 **sānbù nǚrén**

Born in modest circumstances, these women know that money does not grow on trees.

They refuse:

- to compete socially with others (攀比 **pānbǐ**)
- to follow like sheep (盲从 **mángcóng**)
- to stroll about the streets shopping (逛街 **guàngjiē**)

In a frenzied consumer society, these working girls are aware of the value of money and won't be duped. They are unmoved by the sirens of marketing, still less by bling. They believe that "you cannot tell from the outside if the bun contains meat" (包子有肉，不在褶上。 **bāozi yǒu ròu bù zài zhěshàng**)—in other words, all that glitters is not gold.

The "3 No's" Women prefer to consume sensibly. They are very resourceful and being computer virtuosos they prefer Internet shopping to wasting time in over-crowded stores. Their pragmatism is peerless when it comes to making every yuan go a long way. The "3 No's" Women are true gems for their future husband.

Just for the fun of it, the three particularities of the "3 No's" Woman have been interpreted as:

- She is not looking for money (不指望钱 **bù zhǐ wàng qián**)
- She has no high expectations (没有太大期望 **méiyǒu tàidà qīwàng**)
- She does not get on your nerves (不纠结 **bù jiūjié**)

## ■ The "Carnivore" Woman (also called the "Carnivore" or the "Carnivorous" Woman)

食肉女 shíròu nǚ

The concept of the "Carnivore" Woman comes from Japan and refers to a financially independent woman without a life partner. This tribe is made up of disparate profiles ranging from the timid, who only reluctantly ventures from her cocoon, to the glamorous, trend-setting fashionista, as elegant as a butterfly.

Marriage being a key traditional value, the "Carnivore" Woman is driven by a desire to swap her single life for a duet, and to nestle in the hollow of a tender and reassuring shoulder.

But it is no easy matter when their male counterparts "are in no hurry to marry at the age of 20, not in a panic about it at 30, and monopolized by their careers at 40."

The "Carnivores'" key principle is crystal clear: men and women are equal in their quest to find true love. As a result, "Carnivores" may take the initiative, convinced that their prince charming merely forgot their door code number.

Is the "Carnivore" Woman an angel or a demon?

## ■ The *Shengnu* (also called the "Woman Who Remains Alone" or the "Leftover" Woman)
剩女 **shèngnǚ**

In a country with a demographic imbalance like China's, with 105 men for every 100 women, the "women who remain single" are neither surplus nor superfluous. As a group they have adopted the banner of the "Three S" Women: Single, born in the Seventies, and Stuck alone. They have a "high salary" (高薪 **gāo xīn**), a "high level of education" (高学历 **gāo xuélì**), and a "high professional position" (高职位 **gāo zhíwèi**).

The unconventional "Still Single" Women feed public debate, as they are puzzling to a society where marriage is a key value.

Over time, "Still Single" Women go through several stages, from novice to a respected position:

Between the age of 23 or 24, "you see her and you like her" (人见人爱 **rén jiàn rén ài**). The "Still Single" Woman is portrayed as an "abandoned tomato" (剩女果 **shèngnǚ guǒ**) in a phonetic pun with "cherry tomato" (圣女果 **shèngnǚ guǒ**), since she is still "good enough to eat." Being single and financially independent, this go-getting bachelorette cherishes her freedom. She has no taste for short-term love affairs, or for long-term celibacy. Her heart is for the taking and she "aspires after happiness, just like trees long for the advent of spring" (人望幸福，树望春。 **rén wàng xìngfú, shù wàng chūn**). But deep inside, she knows that "striking it lucky" (finding the right husband) is as rare as hen's teeth. Her motto appears to be: "Better be alone than in bad company" (与恶友交不如独处。 **yǔ èyǒu jiāo bùrú dúchù**). At this age, she has certainly been offered the best-selling Chinese novel, *A Story of Du Lala's Promotion*. In this book, the leading character is a young woman from humble roots who manages a spectacular career track. She offers precious advice to young women seeking professional success.

Between the ages of 25 and 27, the "Still Single" Woman sets out to find her kindred spirit. She resembles an epic "abandoned knight" (剩骑士 **shèng qíshì**), which is pronounced just like the "Sacred Knight" (圣骑士 **shèng qíshì**) of a popular Japanese Manga called the Knights of the Zodiac.

Between the ages of 28 and 30, the "Still Single" Woman becomes one who will "certainly remain alone" (必剩客 **bì shèngkè**), a phonetic pun that has the same pronunciation but the opposite meaning of "Pizza Hut" (必胜客 **bì shèngkè**), the "one who will certainly win." At this age, the "Still Single" Woman incarnates the "Abandoned Zodiac Fighter"

(剩斗士 **shèngdòushì**), another melodious play on words with the Saint Seiya, called the "Sacred Zodiac Fighter" (圣斗士 **shèngdòushì**).

Between the ages of 31 and 35, the "Still Single" Woman joins the elite "Abandoned Battle Buddha" (斗战剩佛 **dòuzhàn shèngfó**), which is a phonetic play on words with "Battle Mystic Buddha" (斗战圣佛 **dòuzhàn shèngfó**), a title of the Monkey

King in the popular classic tale, *Journey to the West*.

Beyond the age of 35, she becomes the "Great Abandoned, Equal of Heaven" (齐天大剩 **qítiān-dàshèng**), with reference to another title conferred on the Monkey King. With his super-powers and his brilliant mind, he caused havoc in heaven by fomenting a rebellion to overthrow the establishment. After much trouble, the Emperor of Heaven promoted him to the status of the "Great Sage, Equal of Heaven" (齐天大圣 **qítiāndàshèng**) in an attempt to mollify him.

Once she has blown out 45 candles on her birthday cake, the "Still Single" Woman reaches the ultimate stage. She may be perceived as a "saint" (圣女 **shèng nǚ**) and (why not?) the "winner" of a perfect independence (胜女 **shèng nǚ**).

In China, just like in many developed countries, the number of unmarried men and women keeps increasing. This phenomenon is not peculiar to Chinese society.

> 月下老人，你是不是把我的红线玩断了？
> **yuèxià lǎorén, nǐ shì bú shì bǎ wǒ de hóngxiàn wánduàn le?**
> Matchmaker, have you played with the red string and broke it?

The old man under the Moon is the Chinese Matchmaker (see story on pages 84–85).

## ■ The "Dried-fish" Woman (also called the "Dried-fish" Lady)
干物女 **gānwù nǚ**

This colloquial expression comes from a Japanese TV series, *Hotaru no Hikari* (Glow of Fireflies), about a young woman navigating between professional success and emotional desert.

Popularized in China, the "Dried-fish" Woman conveys the image of a model employee who has a preference for a peaceful life and a daily routine. She does not exist for other people and she has nothing to prove. Her motto could be "I am as I am, take me or leave me."

She aspires to a life without shadows and clouds. Her lethargy, too, is a shield protecting her from constraints and commitments. She seems to be telling people around her, "I'm no Mona Lisa, I can't smile at everyone" (我不是蒙娜丽莎，没办法对谁都微笑。**wǒ búshì méngnàlìshā, méi bànfǎ duì shéi dōu wēixiào**).

It is possible to describe some "Dried-fish" Women as indifferent, with no ideals and no beliefs:

| 冷无缺 lěng wú quē | | |
|---|---|---|
| 冷 | 无 | 缺 |
| **冷**漠 | **无**理想 | 信仰**缺**失 |
| **LĚNG**mò | **WÚ** lǐxiang | xìnyǎng **QUĒ**shī |
| indifferent | no ideals | no beliefs |

Where affairs of the heart are concerned, she has eliminated all the annoyance inherent in romance and will think twice before putting on the old ball and chain. She is certainly not ready to exchange her freedom for a bowl of noodles. She is aware that "one false step can lead to everlasting regret" (一失足成千古恨 **yìshīzú chéng qiāngǔhèn**).

This homebird gets along with her opposite, the "high protein," vitamin-enhanced tornado who sees life rather like a boxing ring and kick-starts everyone with her energetic approach.

你愿意和我结婚吗？
**nǐ yuànyì hé wǒ jiéhūn ma?**
Will you marry me?

非常艰难的决定。
**fēicháng jiānnán de juédìng.**
That's a difficult decision to make.

The expression "That's a difficult decision to make" caused a buzz on the Internet.

She was deeply moved but afterwards she rejected him:
十动然拒 **shí dòng rán jù**

| 十动然拒 shí dòng rán jù |
|---|
| These 4 Chinese characters are the abbreviation of a sentence: **She was deeply moved but afterwards she rejected him.** |
| 十分感动，然后拒绝。<br>**SHÍfèn gǎnDÒNG, RÁNhòu JÙjué.** |

73

## ■ The "Peacock" Woman
### 孔雀女 kǒngquè nǚ

Fairy godmothers must have waved a wand over the cradles of the "Peacocks." They are raised by well-off families in the cities and are the apple of their parents' eyes. They enjoy a trouble-free existence at the center of a galaxy that gravitates around them.

There is no single "Peacock" profile. While some may prefer that their "Prince Charming" (白马王子 **BáiMǎWángzǐ**) arrives with a **BMW**, others believe that money is not an essential criteria in their search for an ideal husband. For a "Peacock," the foundations for a lasting relationship are rectitude and trust.

> 红酒奶酪减肥法。
> **hóngjiǔ nǎilào jiǎn féifǎ.**
> Red wine and cheese are a way of losing weight.

## ■ The "No-No" Woman
### 没女 méi nǚ

This neologism stems from a South Korean TV series entitled *My Name is Kim Sam Soon*, whose heroine is a very ordinary woman. It became very popular in China and the "No-No" Woman now incarnates a curvaceous single woman in her 30s. By phonetic coincidence, "beautiful woman" (美女 **měi nǚ**) sounds like its exact opposite, the "no-no woman" (没女 **méi nǚ**). She has no dream figure, no wealth, and she doesn't stand out. In fact she is a "noodles in broth" (清汤挂面 **qīngtāng guàmiàn**) woman, meaning someone devoid of frivolity. Her dress code might be described as apparently effortless, and emphasizes her unadorned and natural look. Does not tradition say that "internal beauty is valued over external appearance" (心灵美胜过外表 **xīnlíng měi shèngguò wàibiǎo**)?

This type of woman is gaining popularity today, since many people regard kindness as attractive.

## ■ The "37°" Woman (also called the "Everyman's Dream" Woman)
### 37°女人/37度女人 **37° nǚrén/37dù nǚrén**

The "37°" Woman is the name of a magazine. It also refers to a woman with natural elegance and sophistication.

Away from the dictates of fashion, she asserts her personal style with confidence. The "37°" Woman carefully selects her own wardrobe to best suit her figure and to show herself in the best light. The passing of time does not diminish her beauty and she is second to none when it comes to letting "charm" (魅力 **mèilì**) blend with "beauty" (美丽 **měilì**).

The "37°" Woman has an iron fist in a kid glove. She considers that speech is silver and silence is golden, perfectly embodying the notion of "soft" power. She knows how to strike a happy medium and her wise advice is well-appreciated among her friends.

The "37°" Woman symbolizes the ideal woman. Her 37 degrees can be made up as follows: 10 for wisdom, 10 for charm, 10 for charisma, and 7 for refinement.

The "37°" Man has also appeared in dictionaries. How would you define him?

## ■ The "Perfect" Woman
### 白富美 báifùměi

In 2012 a new buzzword appeared on the Internet to describe the perfect woman. It is a combination of three words:

| 白富美 báifùměi | | |
|---|---|---|
| Pale complexion 白 bái | Rich 富 fù | Beautiful 美 měi |

These three characteristics can be interpreted as follows:

- A pale complexion that symbolizes elegance (白于品行 bái yú pǐnxíng)
- "Rich" refers to the intellect (富于思维 fù yú sīwéi)
- "Beautiful" refers to sharp mindedness (美在心灵 měi zài xīnlíng)

But a play on words produces a completely different result:

| 白富美 báifùměi | | |
|---|---|---|
| 白 bái | 富 fù | 美 měi |
| 白痴 báichī | 富态 fùtai | 臭美 chòuměi |
| Stupid | Obese | Conceited |

## ■ The *DAMA* (or "big mother/aunt")
### 中国大妈 zhōngguó dàmā

大妈 **dàmā** can be translated as Big MAMA or Mother. It is usually used for women over 40. The rich middle-age women particularly appreciate "open air dancing" (广场舞 **guǎngchǎng wǔ**). They take great care of the family money and purchase gold jewelry since, in their eyes, it represents a profitable investment. They have attracted worldwide attention as they have contributed to the high price of gold.

> 大妈是主力军买金如同买白菜！
> **dà mā shì zhǔ lì jūn mǎi jīn rú tóng mǎi báicài !**
> DAMA is the main driving force to buy gold
> just like buying cabbage!

*–China News Daily*, May 2013

## ■ The "Manly" Woman (also called the "Fe(male)")
### 女汉子 nǚ hànzǐ

The term 女汉子 **nǚ hànzǐ** has been created for an independent lady who does not rely on men for her existence. This courageous woman is often portrayed with muscles and described as having the "strength of a bull"(力大如牛 **lìdà rú niú**). The fact is that she does not behave in a traditional feminine way and she would, for instance, never behave like a spoiled child and spend hours looking at herself in a mirror. The "Manly" Woman does not believe in the old idiomatic expression "marry a chicken and follow a chicken, marry a dog and follow a dog" (嫁鸡随鸡，嫁狗随狗。 **jià jī suí jī, jià gǒu suí gǒu**). She likes to "fight on her own" (独

自奋斗 **dúzì fèndòu**). Her slogan is for sure "be yourself"(做你自己 **zuò nǐ zìjǐ**).

Here are some traits of the "Manly" Woman:

- She speaks out her mind in a straightforward way.
- She can fix anything by herself in her flat (including plumbing).
- When traveling she carries her luggage on her own.
- Even if she wears high heels she can run after the bus to be on time for work.
- She considers that putting on make up is annoying, and she does not like to dress up.
- She is single.

> 你长这么漂亮，你家里人知道吗？
> **nǐ zhǎng zhème piàoliàng, nǐ jiālǐrén zhīdào ma?**
> You are so beautiful, your parents know it?

# MODERN-DAY COUPLES

# CUPID AND THE "THREE PRECONDITIONS"

I n China, love at first sight is "a first glance that pierces the heart like a needle." This enchantment can lead a wooer to climb "a mountain of swords and a sea of flames" (上刀山，下火海。**shàng dāoshān, xià huǒhǎi**). With a poetic touch, a romantic idyll is depicted by a pair of birds flying side-by-side, or by two interlaced branches. The lovebirds are represented by "two butterflies flying in the sky, whose shadows never separate" (蝴蝶双飞，形影相随。**húdié shuāng fēi, xíng yǐng xiāng suí**).

Idealized as a path taken by two spouses "until their hair turns white" (白头偕老 **báitóu xiélǎo**), the couple is symbolized by a pair of mandarin ducks representing fidelity. Love is an unwavering complicity that leads to the fusion of the yin and yang energies—promising a long and radiant life—and is part of an unfailing generosity and devotion. This is embodied by the likes of the old man in Jiangjing Province, who dug 6,000 steps in the side of a mountain so that his beloved octogenarian wife could come down from where they live.

The legend goes that every love affair is predestined. It is claimed that couples are listed in a lengthy register kept by the "old man in the moonlight" (月下老人 **yuèxiàlǎorén**). He wears a tunic and sports a long white beard, and his mission is to tie together the lovers' feet with a long, red silk thread—wherever they may be in the world, and whatever their social origin.

The concept of "destiny" (缘分 **yuánfèn**) is still deeply rooted in China today. Nevertheless, it appears that people prefer a perfect match with the girl or boy "of the opposite door" (门当户对 **méndānghùduì**)—that is to say, from the same social

The Chinese equivalent of Cupid is an old man
who catches his prey with red silk ties.

background. Another saying, "the man works outside and the woman stays at home" (男主外，女主内。**nán zhǔ wài, nǚ zhǔ nèi**), remains a model for many couples.

While men may seek the perfect housewife, women seek an ambitious, hardworking, and protective husband. A common saying has it that "men are afraid to choose the wrong profession, while women are afraid to choose the wrong husband" (男怕入错行，女怕嫁错郎。**nán pà rù cuò háng, nǚ pà jià cuò láng**).

Popular wisdom dictates that three prerequisites are necessary to succeed in married life. They are known as the "three major items" (三大件 **sān dà jiàn**) and have evolved with time:

- In the 1970s: a watch, a bicycle, and a sewing machine
- In the 1980s: a color TV, a fridge, and a washing machine
- In the 1990s: an apartment, a car, air conditioning
- In the 2000s: an apartment, a car, and banknotes

## "Drinking the wine of happiness"

Marriage is happiness shared by two and is symbolized by a special character, composed of the word "happiness" (喜 **xǐ**) doubled for the occasion.

Happiness is expressed through a young married couple.

### "The Old Man in the Moonlight"—also called "the Old Man Under the Moon" (the Chinese equivalent of Cupid)

At the time of the Tang Dynasty, a young man called Wei Gu visited a town called Songchen and found lodgings at an inn. In the evening he went for a stroll in the streets. Under the moon, he observed an old man sitting on the floor, immersed in a voluminous book. Nearby was a large bag, overflowing with red silk strings.

As he approached the old man, Wei Gu realized with surprise that the pages were blank. Burning with curiosity, he ventured to ask what this strange book was about.

With a broad smile the old man replied that it was a magical register of all the world's marriages. Wei Gu then enquired about the utility of the red strings. The old man explained that it was for tying the feet of lovers made for each other. Once tied, whatever their social status, or wherever they were in the world, they could not escape their destiny. With a mischievous smile, he added that he was very careful to catch them just at the moment they least expected it.

Wei Gu had some doubts about the words of this old man, but accompanied him to the market. On their way they passed a blind woman carrying a baby girl in her arms. "That baby," said the old man, "will be your future wife," and he went on to tell him that the wedding would take place in 17 years' time. Wei Gu grew angry, convinced that the man was making fun of him. He ordered a servant to go and kill the child. He then went looking for the old man, but he had vanished as if by magic.

Nearly two decades passed and Wei Gu married the daughter of a nobleman. She was extremely beautiful, her delicate looks marred only by a tiny scar between her brows. When Wei Gu asked his father-in-law about the scar, he was told that 17 years earlier in Songchen, a servant had taken his daughter to the market. Suddenly, for no reason at all, someone had struck the child with a sword and then fled. Fortunately the child was safe and sound, but the attack had left a small scar.

Wei Gu felt disconcerted when he remembered the events. Pale-faced, he asked his father-in-law if the child's servant at the time was blind. Surprised in turn, his father-in-law confirmed that she was. Wei Gu was dumbstruck for a few minutes and then, full of shame and remorse, told his father-in-law the whole story. The kind nobleman forgave him.

The story spread throughout the region and since that time everyone knows that an invisible hand is at work to unite men and women. However, since nobody knew the name of the old matchmaker, he has been called "the old man in the moonlight," and the inn in Songchen where Wei Gu stayed has been named "the engagement inn."

Wedding ceremonies vary from region to region, but some elements are common. The couple must first register their marriage by law at the city hall. Witnesses are optional. Once married, the couple hand out sweets to their relatives and colleagues. A few weeks or even months later, they may hold a banquet to celebrate their union. Favorite dates are the 6th, 16th and 26th of the month, as these numbers are auspicious.

The marriage festivities, known as "drinking the wine of happiness" (喝喜酒 **hē xǐjiǔ**), start in the morning, since the afternoon is usually reserved for the second wedding ceremony. The groom goes to fetch his bride at her home. He is greeted by her friends, who tease him and form a human barrier to prevent him from entering. The groom is pushed back. He will insist

and persuade them to let him in to get his bride, whose shoes have been carefully hidden to prevent her from slipping away. To force his way in, he will distribute red envelopes containing a small amount of cash, depending on his financial situation. He should, however, not be stingy. He may also offer cigarettes.

Once the groom has found his bride they set off to the party venue. A professional master of ceremonies may also be hired for the occasion. The bride will wear a traditional red dress or a white, Western-style one, and may frequently change dresses during the photo session.

Custom has it that during the ceremony the bride should be moved to tears to mark her departure from her home, since from that day on she will join her husband's family. In line with tradition, she will serve tea to the parents of her husband. The engagement may be sealed with the words, "Seas may dry out and rocks may crumble to dust, but I will always be loyal to you" (海枯石烂，不变心。 **hǎikūshílàn, bú biànxīn**).

Those who only register their wedding at the Civil Status and Identification Service opt for what is commonly known as a "naked marriage" (裸婚 **luǒ hūn**). They have no car, no apartment, and avoid extravagant spending for the ceremony.

For others, a wedding is an exceptional moment and the ceremony must take place in a spectacular location, such as the tropical island of Hainan, or the city of Zhuhai in Guangdong province, regarded as China's most romantic city.

## Cultural tips

Do you know the hidden meaning behind offering lilies to a young married couple? The lily is called 百合 **bǎihé** in Chinese, which can be interpreted as a contraction of "a hundred years of harmony"(百年好合 **bǎinián hǎohé**).

Guess why dates, peanuts, laurel and melon seeds are placed on the young couple's bridal bed? It is easy to guess why, thanks to the homophones and the associated good fortune:

| dates | peanuts | laurel | melon seeds |
|---|---|---|---|
| 枣 **ZǍO** | 花生 **huāSHĒNG** | 桂圆 **GUÌ yuán** | 瓜子 **guāZǏ** |

| quickly | give birth | to a child |
|---|---|---|
| 早 **zǎo** | 生 **shēng** | 贵子 **guì zǐ** |

## The Butterfly Lovers
## (the Chinese equivalent of Romeo and Juliet)

A long time ago, in a valley of Sichuan Province, lived the young Yingtai. She was the only girl in a family of nine and charmed everyone with her beauty and wit. She cherished her freedom and managed to throw off all her suitors. With her thirst for knowledge, her only dream was to study, even though education was a privilege reserved for men.

As she grew older, the intrepid Yingtai managed with patience and persistence to convince her father, a nobleman, to let her be disguised as a young man and leave home to pursue her studies. Away from home, she met Shanbo, an intelligent and charming young man from a humble background. They grew very fond of each other and became so inseparable that they made a binding oath. For four years they sat at the same desk and shared the same room. This was a time of bliss for Yingtai, who fell in love with the young man, while he, for his part, was quite unaware that his dear friend was a woman.

One day Yingtai received a letter from her father asking her to return home. Before leaving, she confided her secret to the

After a few years of marriage, the husband and wife give each other a "love lock" (同心锁 **tóngxīnsuǒ**). Legend has it that a young woman from a rich family fell in love with a poor man. Since the young woman's parents were opposed to their marriage, the lovers fled to the top of a mountain and jumped off, so as to stay together forever. The only thing that remained of them was a lock.

A love lock

headmaster's wife and presented her with a jade pendant to give to Shanbo. Tormented by her feelings, she decided to attempt to confess the truth before she left but being afraid of his reaction, she couched her words in so many metaphors that poor Shanbo failed to understand her meaning. She finally invented a beautiful sister who closely resembled her and promised to give him her hand in marriage, which Shanbo accepted.

When Shanbo later learnt that his sworn brother and her "sister" were one and the same, he was filled with joy. But their common dream of happiness was short-lived. Yingtai's father had already arranged that she would marry a rich nobleman, and nothing could make him change his plans. Shanbo fell into despair and died of a broken heart.

On the day of her wedding, Yingtai passed in front of Shanbo's final resting place and knelt down to pay her respects. At this moment, black clouds veiled the Sun and the grave opened up. Yingtai unhesitatingly leaped into it. The clouds immediately dissipated and the sky brightened again. The following day with the first rays of dawn, two butterflies were seen flying out of the tomb, dancing into the blue sky.

## Wedding reception games

### Sweets

The groom has his hands tied behind his back and has to pick up 12 sweets with his mouth while the guests look on. He mustn't swallow the sweets, but every time he picks one up he has to say, "My wife, I love you." In the end he has to spit them all out onto a plate and if any are missing, one of the guests may ask him to start all over again.

### The Tender Heart

The groom lies down with slices of banana all over his face and neck. The bride, blindfolded and with her hands tied behind her back, has to find all the slices and eat them without letting one fall to the ground. If one should fall, she has to drink a glass of wine. She may, however, ask her best friend to represent her in this.

## Mobile Phone

The bride places a mobile phone in the groom's right hand sleeve, then she has to move it across to the other sleeve. When the telephone reaches his heart, one of the guests will call on the phone and she has to answer while continuing the game.

## Wedding Rings

For this game a large ice cube is prepared beforehand from honey, water, and spices, with the rings set inside it. With their hands tied behind their backs, the couple has to get through to the rings by licking or biting the ice cube. The

first one to get a ring must shout out, "I love you" and give it to his/her partner, who will respond with a kiss to the applause of the assembled guests.

## Tasty Glasses

Five glasses of water are prepared with each of the "five flavors" (五味 **wǔ wèi**): salty, sour, spicy, bitter, and sweet. The couple has to drink them all but they are allowed to hold their noses if they wish.

### The Balloons

Six single men and women each write a few words about one of the guests and slip it into a balloon. The men then blow up all the balloons until they burst and read the comments out loud.

### The Kiss

The women guests must kiss a sheet of paper and the groom has to try to recognize his wife's kiss among all the lipstick kisses.

## The golden rules

In the old days, a woman had to respect the "Three Submissions and Four Virtues," also called the "Three Obediences and the Four Virtues" (三从四德 **sāncóngsìdé**).

She had to submit to her father, then to her husband, and if widowed, to her son (the "Three Submissions"), while respecting the virtues of morality, proper speech, modesty, and diligences (the "Four Virtues").

In China today gender equality is enshrined in the law and a husband is supposed to share his income—bonuses included—with his wife. The main stated qualities for spouses are listed in

manuals of social etiquette, on local government websites, and even in guides for new residents.

A wife should be lenient with her husband and cultivate good relations with her mother-in-law. Her "other half" must be considerate (for instance, by helping with domestic tasks and remembering his wife's birthday), and never forget to tell his beloved when he is working late.

Despite all this advice, life is uncertain and marriage may turn out to be a long road full of pitfalls. As if to corroborate this, a movie called *The Cell Phone* caused quite a stir. In this story, a woman discovers, through her husband's cell phone, that he is cheating on her. New technology, it seems, is an open invitation for men to commit infidelity, lured by the irresistible sirens called "private secretaries."

To prevent a passion from dying or fading away, various "anti boredom" methods are employed. One sign of the times is that the number of "trial marriages" (试婚 **shìhūn**), divorces, and cohabitation is on the increase ....

# Modern-Day Tribes

## ■ The Couple from "Only-Child Families"
独生夫妻 dúshēng fūqī

The government's birth control policy has exerted a considerable impact on family structure. One of the major consequences is that young people bear greater responsibility for the whole family.

The spouses of married couples from only-child families never cease to juggle their commitments, trying to reach a delicate balance between married life and filial duty. During traditional celebrations, they have to run from one set of in-laws to the other. Throughout the year they keep an eye on their elders,

and, as often as possible, support them financially as well.

As a result of the generational imbalance, people aged 60 and above represent 14 percent of the population, compared with 17 percent for the under 14 year-olds. This has given rise to debates on the birth control and generated a relaxation of the rules of the one child policy in 2014.

## ■ The "Half Candy" Couple (also called the "Half-sweet" Couple or the "Half-sugared" Couple)
半糖夫妻 **bàntáng fūqī**

This neologism comes from a popular song, which advises couples not to stay "glued together" and preserve their own vital space. Unlike the "Migratory Birds" (侯鸟夫妻 **hòuniǎo fūqī**) who have to live apart because of their professional activities and only meet at weekends, the "Half Candy" Couples are separated by choice. Their aim is to demonstrate their mutual trust and to avoid their love life descending into a routine.

This is a good example of a "Champagne" Couple—those who wants to preserve the bubbles and excitement of the early days.

## ■ The "DINK" Couple
丁克 **dīngkè**

"Double Income No Kids" is a social phenomenon that exists throughout the world. For these couples, life without a toddler can also be happy, and the pleasures of giving birth, sterilizing baby bottles, and changing diapers do not cross their minds. Becoming "child slaves" (孩奴 **háinú**) is not their dream.

A happy child-free couple

DINK goes against the cliché of women becoming fulfilled by motherhood; but one consequence is the potential tension between a mother-in-law who wants to preserve the family's lineage, and a daughter-in-law with a strong taste for freedom.

With their fertile imaginations, netizens have created other acronyms to describe the lives of couples:

- The DINKWAD—Double Income No Kids With A Dog (丁狗族 **dīnggǒu zú**)

- The DINKEM—Double Income No Kids With Excessive Mortgage (丁 啃 **dīngkěn**)

- The DINS—Double Income No Sex (丁士族 **dīngshì zú**) This acronym comes from Taiwan and describes couples so immersed in their professional lives that their desire has vanished.

They can be described by one expression: they "do not have any relation anymore and they do not get divorced" (一不做 二不休 **yī bú zuò èr bú xiū**). With a beautiful rhyme, they will tell you that "love forever does not exist" (天长地久， 根本没有。 **tiānchángdìjiǔ, gēnběn méiyǒu**). And for them

"marriage has turned out to be the grave of love" (婚姻是
爱情的坟墓。 **hūnyīn shì àiqíng de fénmù**).

■ The New DINKs (新丁克 **xīn dīngkè**)
These couples do not want to abandon the idea of having a
child, but ask for the support of their parents.

■ The DINK Exit Tribe/Clan (悔丁族 **huǐdīng zú**)
The couples who have given in and have joined the ranks of
parents.

**PART 2**

# WORD PLAY:
How It Reveals Today's
Chinese Mind

**B** y decoding characters we understand their magic and their secrets. The examples below are for pleasure, rather than a true linguistic interpretation.

## Chinese Characters and Matters of the Heart

- What suggests a "heart in autumn"?

| 心 xīn | + | 秋 qiū | = | 愁 chóu |
|---|---|---|---|---|
| "Heart" | | "Autumn" | | "Worry about something/being anxious" |

- What does a "heart caught in a door" mean?

| 心 xīn | + | 门 mén | = | 闷 mèn |
|---|---|---|---|---|
| "Heart" | | "Door" | | "Bored" |

- What lies behind the character "to marry"?

| 女 nǚ | + | 昏 hūn | = | 婚 hūn |
|---|---|---|---|---|
| "Woman" | | "Muddled" | | "To marry" |

- Is kissing a taboo?

| 口 kǒu | + | 勿 wù | = | 吻 wěn |
|---|---|---|---|---|
| "Mouth" | | "Do not" | | "Kissing" |

- May love be interpreted as a "weird emotion"?

| 变 biàn + 态 tài | = | 变态 biàn tài | = | 恋 liàn |
|---|---|---|---|---|
| "Altered state" | | "Abnormal" | | "Love" |

- What does a "blade associated with a heart" stand for?

| 刃 rèn | + | 心 xīn | = | 忍 rěn |
|---|---|---|---|---|
| "Blade" | | "Heart" | | "To endure" |

- What is the meaning of an "upside down heart"?

| 心 xīn | + | 上 shàng | + 下 xià | = | 忐忑不安 |
|--------|---|----------|---------|---|---------|
| "Heart" | | "Underneath" | "On top" | | **tǎntè bù'ān** |
| | | | | | "Ill at ease" |

Here are some more examples:

| 田 tián | + | 力 lì | = | 男 nán |
|---------|---|-------|---|--------|
| "Field" | | "Strength" | | "Man" |

| 雨 yǔ | + | 田 tián | = | 雷 léi |
|-------|---|---------|---|--------|
| "Rain" | | "Field" | | "Thunder" |

| 日 rì | + | 生 shēng | = | 星 xīng |
|-------|---|----------|---|--------|
| "Sun" | | "To be born" | | "A star" |

# Drawing Characters Creatively: Word-drawings on the Internet

Characters may be drawn as illustrations—here are some examples widely disseminated on the Internet (chinese-tools. com). New ones are constantly being created.

爱 **ai**
An elaborate drawing for "love"

This is how to draw a little rascal from the three characters that make up the word in Chinese.

坏小孩 **huài xiǎohái**
A little rascal or a little imp?

**103**

熊猫 **xióngmāo**
A panda (literally a "bear-cat")

美丽的姑娘 **měilì de gūniang**
A beautiful young lady

# Melodious Homophones

## Good luck or bad luck?

Many numbers and words have underlying meanings. Here are a few well-known examples:

| 六 **liù** | 六六大顺 **liùliù dàshùn** |
|---|---|
| Number 6 | Everything will go smoothly |

The number 6 suggests that everything is fine, so the expression means "all is well" (i.e., everything happens for the best).

| 八 **bā** | 发财 **fācái** |
|---|---|
| Number 8 | To make a fortune/to get rich |

The number 8 (八 **bā**) is associated with good fortune because it sounds much like **fā** ("to prosper") in Cantonese. If you seek a lucky time to start a business, it will be ideally on the 8th day of the month at 8 AM. Remember that the Olympic Games in China opened on August 8, 2008, at 8 minutes past 8 in the morning.

The slogan "Beijing welcomes you" (北京欢迎你 **Běijīng huānyíng nǐ**) was made up of the names of each of the mascots for the Games: **Bei**bei, **Jing**jing, **Huan**huan, **Ying**ying, and **Ni**ni.

| 九 **jiǔ** | 久 **jiǔ** |
|---|---|
| Number 9 | Eternity/long |

The number 9 sounds like "eternity." It was reported in the newspapers that a lover once offered 999 roses to his girlfriend. There are regular reports of people paying vast sums of money at auctions for telephone numbers and car number plates with a sequence of lucky numbers (i.e., 6, 8 and 9).

| 蝠 **fú** | 福 **fú** |
|---|---|
| Bat | Good fortune |

The "bat" has the same pronunciation as "good fortune." This is why bats are so frequently represented on decorative objects.

| 苹果 **píngguǒ** | 平 **píng** |
|---|---|
| Apple | Peace/calm |

The word for "apple" in Chinese has the same tonal intonation as "safe and sound" in Chinese (平安 **píng'ān**), and apples have therefore come to symbolize safety—to the extent that people put real or fake ones in their cars to protect themselves from road accidents.

| 鹿 **lù**<br>Deer/stag | 禄 **lù**<br>Salary |
| --- | --- |

The word for "deer/stag" sounds like the word for "salary" (it was originally the term for "an official's pay"). So if you offer as a gift a statue of a deer, this implies, in a subtle way, that you wish your friend a promotion or a pay rise!

| 喜鹊 **xǐquè**<br>Magpie | 喜 **xǐ**<br>Happiness |
| --- | --- |

The magpie is literally the "bird that brings happiness." The Chinese believe that "when magpies are calling, they must have good news" (喜鹊见好事到。 **xǐquè jiàn hǎoshì dào**).

| 分梨 **fēn lí**<br>To cut a pear in half | 分离 **fēnlí**<br>To separate/to part from each other |
| --- | --- |

It is ill-advised for a couple to cut pears in half. Indeed, it is pronounced the same way as separation!

| 三 **sān**<br>The number 3 | 散 **sàn**<br>To break up |
| --- | --- |

Number 3 sounds very much like the words for "break up."

| 钟 **zhōng** | 终 **zhōng** |
|---|---|
| Clock | Make funeral arrangements |

It is ominous to offer someone a "clock" since it sounds like "making funeral arrangements."

| 四 **sì** | 死 **sǐ** |
|---|---|
| Number 4 | Death |

Number "4" brings bad luck, since it has the same tonal intonation as "to die." Needless to say, some hotels and hospitals avoid having a fourth floor or a room number four.

福星 fúxīng          禄星 lùxīng          寿星 shòuxīng

The three lucky Taoist star gods are very popular in China.
They are the "star of happiness" (福星 fúxīng), the "star of good fortune" (禄星 lùxīng), and the "star of longevity" (寿星 shòuxīng).

# Twisted Meanings

The meanings of many common expressions can be changed while keeping the same pronunciation, or one very close to it.

| Original meaning | Twisted meaning |
|---|---|
| 研究生 **yánjiūshēng**<br>A graduate student | 烟酒生 **yān jiǔ shēng**<br>An expert in alcohol and cigarettes |
| 幸福 **xìngfú**<br>Happiness | 性福 **xìngfú**<br>Sexual pleasure |
| 主妇 **zhǔfù**<br>Housewife | 煮夫 **zhǔ fū**<br>A husband who cooks |
| 富翁 **fùwēng**<br>A millionaire | 负翁 **fùwēng**<br>A person heavily laden with debts |
| 改邪归正 **gǎi xié guī zhèng**<br>Turning over a new leaf (to give up evil and return to virtue) | 改鞋归正 **gǎi xié guī zhèng**<br>Changing one's shoes and following the straight path |
| 气管炎 **qìguǎnyán**<br>Bronchitis | 妻管炎 **qīguǎnyán**<br>A hen-pecked husband |

## Some amusing constructions

- Luck is a cloud that appears to pass by in silence.

| 云 **yún**<br>Cloud | 运 **yùn**<br>Luck |
|---|---|

- "Make-up" sounds like "pretense."

| 化妆 huàzhuāng | 化装 huà zhuāng |
|---|---|
| To make oneself up | To disguise oneself |

- The "stock market" sounds like "an ancient poem" or "a story."

| 股市 gǔshì | 古诗 gǔshī | 故事 gùshì |
|---|---|---|
| Stock market | Ancient poetry | A story |

- A "lawyer" may master the art of poetry.

| 律师 lǜshī | 律诗 lǜshī |
|---|---|
| Lawyer | The verse of a poem |

- To be "famous" is just an "illusion."

| 吃香 chīxiāng | 痴想 chīxiǎng |
|---|---|
| To be popular | Wishful thinking/daydreaming |

- "Speculation" is a "crime."

| 投机 tóujī | 偷鸡 tōu jī |
|---|---|
| To speculate | To steal a chicken |

- What are the prerequisites for becoming a "perfect manager"?

| 经理 jīnglǐ | 经历 jīnglì | 精力 jīnglì |
|---|---|---|
| A manager | Experience | Energy |

- What is the hidden meaning of "ambition"?

| 抱负 bàofù | 暴富 bàofù |
|---|---|
| Ambition | Get rich quick |

- To make "a splash" when you fall into the water rhymes with "I do not understand."

| 扑通 **pūtōng** | 不懂 **bù dǒng** |
|---|---|
| Splash in the water | I do not understand |

- A "microblogging" site shares something in common with a "scarf."

| 微博 **wēibó** | 围脖 **wéibó** |
|---|---|
| Microblog | Scarf |

And by extension, "to knit a scarf" (织围脖 **zhī wéibó**) now means "to microblog" (是微博 **shi wēibó**), while someone addicted to microblogging is called a 微博控 **wēibó kòng**.

Here are some other examples of alternative interpretations:

| Original meaning | Twisted meaning |
|---|---|
| 美丽动人 **měilì dòng rén**<br>Beauty excites passion (which means to be loving) | 美丽冻人 **měilì dòng rén**<br>Beauty freezes you |
| 才貌双全<br>**cáimàoshuāngquán**<br>Talent and beauty (two previous advantages when starting out in life) | 财貌双全<br>**cáimàoshuāngquán**<br>Wealth and beauty (two present-day advantages when starting out in life) |

● What does a "blank page" mean?

| Original meaning | Twisted meaning |
|---|---|
| 白纸当然无字了! | 白痴当然无耻了! |
| **báizhǐ dāngrán wúzì le!** | **báichī dāngrán wúchǐ le!** |
| A blank page obviously has no words on it! | An idiot is obviously shameless! |

● "A couple" (夫妻 **fūqī**) may rhyme with "joy" (福气 **fúqì**), but after a few years passion wanes and the spouses see each other differently.

| Original meaning | Twisted meaning |
|---|---|
| 相敬如宾 **xiāngjìng rú bīn** | 相敬如冰 **xiāngjìng rú bīng** |
| Treat each other with respect | Treat each other coldly |

Some sayings have been revisited:

| Original meaning | Transformed meaning |
|---|---|
| 别亲我，我怕羞。<br>**bié qīn wǒ, wǒ pà xiū.**<br>Do not kiss me, I am shy. | 别亲我，我怕修。<br>**bié qīn wǒ, wǒ pà xiū.**<br>Do not bump into me, I am scared of repairs. (This sticker is sometimes seen on the back of cars.) |

Poetry and wisdom can be ambiguous. Here are two cult expressions:

| Original meaning | Twisted meaning |
|---|---|
| 世上无难事，只怕有心人。<br>**shìshàng wú nánshì, zhǐ pà yǒu xīnrén.**<br>Nothing on earth is complicated, my only fear is to lack courage. (The equivalent of "Nothing in the world is difficult for one who sets his mind on it.") | 开车无难事，只怕有新人。<br>**kāichē wú nánshì, zhǐ pà yǒu xīnrén.**<br>Driving is not complicated, my only fear is crossing an inexperienced driver. |

| Original meaning | Twisted meaning |
|---|---|
| 给点阳光，我就灿烂。 **gěi diǎn yángguāng, wǒ jiù cànlàn.** Give me an opportunity to express my talents and I will shine. | 给点阳光，我就腐烂。 **gěi diǎn yángguāng, wǒ jiù fǔlàn.** Give me an opportunity to express my talents and I will be rotten (meaning "I will become corrupt"). |

| Original meaning | Twisted meaning |
|---|---|
| 钱能解决的问题，就不是问题。 **qián néng jiějué de wèntí, jiù búshì wèntí.** If money can solve a problem, there is no problem. | 钱不是问题，问题就是没钱。 **qián búshì wèntí, wèntí jiù shì méi qián.** If money is not a problem, not having any is the problem! |

| Original meaning | Twisted meaning |
|---|---|
| 我不下地狱，谁下地狱？ **wǒ bú xià dìyù, shéi xià dìyù?** If I do not go to hell, who will? (In other words, "If I do not roll up my sleeves and get down to it, who will?") | 我不下地狱，谁爱下谁下。 **wǒ bú xià dìyù, shéi ài xià shéi xià.** I do not wish to go to hell, but anyone else who wants to is free to go. |

Changing the characters that compose a word while keeping the same, or approximately the same, pronunciation can convey a different message:

| Original meaning | Twisted meaning |
|---|---|
| 明月几时有？把酒问青天。 **míngyuè jǐshí yǒu? bǎ jiǔ wèn qīngtiān.** "When will the bright moon appear? I ask the sky with a cup of wine in my hand." (a line by a famous Song dynasty poet Su Shi, also known as Su Dongpo) | 明月几时有？抬头信自己。 **míngyuè jǐshí yǒu? táitóu xìn zìjǐ.** When will the bright moon appear? I look up and believe in myself (meaning, "One has to learn to manage on one's own"). |

## More wordplay

Switching characters around can significantly transform the meaning.

会者不难 **huìzhě bù nán**

For he who knows, there are no obstacles.

难者不会 **nánzhě bú huì**

For the ignorant, nothing is possible.

不好说 **bù hǎo shuō**

It is hard to tell (meaning "embarrassing").

说不好 **shuō bù hǎo**

I am unable to say for certain (meaning "not sure").

不说好 **bù shuō hǎo**

It is better to say nothing.

说你行，你就行，不行也行。

**shuō nǐ xíng, ní jiù xíng, bùxíng yě xíng.**

If I decide that you are the person I need, then it is fine. Even if you are incompetent, it is not a problem (meaning that an incompetent person with connections can make it).

说不行，你就不行，行也不行。

**shuō bùxíng, nǐ jiù bùxíng, xíng yě bùxíng.**

If I decide that you are not the person I need, then there is nothing doing. Even if you are competent, it will not change my mind (meaning know-how and skills are not always enough to make it).

不服不行 **bùfú bùxíng**

If you do not obey, it will not work.

# From Common Expression to Advertising Slogan

Teachers and parents alike lament the fact that well-known idiomatic expressions and sayings are being adapted as advertising slogans.

| Expression | Advertising slogan |
| --- | --- |
| 理所当然 **lǐ suǒ dāngrán**<br>Natural/As a matter of course | 礼所当然 **lǐ suǒ dāngrán**<br>To offer a gift is a natural thing (or politeness is natural) |
| 终生无憾<br>**zhōngshēng wúhàn**<br>To have no regrets in life | 终生无汗<br>**zhōngshēng wúhàn**<br>A sweat-free life! (ad for air conditioners) |
| 贤妻良母 **xiánqī liángmǔ**<br>A perfect wife and loving mother | 闲妻良母 **xiánqī liángmǔ**<br>A busy wife and a good mother (ad for a brand of household cleaners) |
| 以貌取人 **yǐmàoqǔrén**<br>Judging by appearances | 衣帽取人 **yī mào qǔ rén**<br>Judging a person by their clothes and hat (ad for a ready-to-wear clothing brand) |
| 仁者见仁，智者见智。<br>**rénzhě jiàn rén, zhìzhě jiàn zhì.**<br>The wise man sees wisdom. (Idiom: different people have different opinions) | 智者见智，智者见质。<br>**zhìzhě jiàn zhì, zhìzhě jiàn zhì.**<br>The wise man sees quality. |

Some expressions and sayings change meaning over time.

| Saying | Original meaning | Twisted meaning |
|---|---|---|
| 无产阶级 **wúchǎnjiējí** | A classless society | To be broke |
| 婆婆太多媳妇难当 **pópo tài duō xífu nán dāng** | To have an omnipresent mother-in-law is hard for the daughter-in-law | Too many bosses is unbearable for a subordinate. |
| 古往今来 **gǔ wǎng jīn lái** | From ancient to modern times | 股往金来 **gǔ wǎng jīn lái** "Making money on the stock market" |

Sometimes changing one character is enough:

| Original meaning | Twisted meaning |
|---|---|
| 一切向前看 **yíqiè xiàng qián kàn** Look forward | 一切向钱看 **yíqiè xiàng qián kàn** Putting money first in everything |

# Chinese Names for Foreign Companies

Many play on words are to be found in the names of foreign companies operating in China. Following the advice of marketing specialists, some of them choose names on the basis of the values that are thought to be important in the eyes of their consumers. Here are a few well-known examples:

| | |
|---|---|
| 家乐福 **jiālèfú**<br>Carrefour (supermarket chain) | Joy and happiness in the family |
| 可口可乐 **kěkǒukělè**<br>Coca-Cola | The drink that gives pleasure |
| 老佛爷 **lǎo fóyé**<br>Galeries Lafayette (department store) | The name is a reference to Cixi, the last Empress of China (1835–1908), as one of her names was "Lao-foye." The word for Buddha, 佛 **fó**, is used as a mark of respect. |
| 宜家**yíjiā**<br>Ikea | Ideal for the home (or the family) |
| 耐克 **nàikè**<br>Nike | Resist/endure obstacles |
| 高盛 **gāoshèng**<br>Goldman Sachs | **Shèng** can be translated as "prosperity" and "flourishing," so the investment bank's Chinese name pledges respectability and a high return. |
| 德勤 **déqín**<br>Deloitte & Touche | The audit and consultancy firm that promises "morality and diligence" |
| 谷歌 **gǔgē**<br>Google | The valley song |

Some companies convey poetic images:

| 露华浓 **lùhuánóng** Revlon | Dew, beauty, wealth |
|---|---|
| 娇兰 **jiāolán** Guerlain | Delicate orchid |
| 标致 **biāozhì** Peugeot | Beauty/beautiful |

Revlon drew its Chinese name from a verse by the famous Tang dynasty poet, Li Bai (also known as Li Bo, 701–762). At the emperor's request, Li Bai wrote an ode to celebrate the beauty of Yang Guifei, which contained the line, "shimmering with the bright spring dew."

## Some amusing tales

### The meaning of life

Clearly men and women don't see things in the same way.

The story goes that if a woman rests her head on a man's shoulder, it's the beginning of a "story" (故事 **gùshì**); whereas if the man does the same, it's more an "accident" (事故 **shìgù**). By switching the characters around, the meaning changes significantly.

## Undress me!

November 11 is Singles Day in China, because the number 1, symbolizing solitude, appears four times. Consequently 11/11/2011 was a very special date, as the number appeared six times. Some young people stripped off for the occasion, because "to get undressed" (脱光 **tuō guāng**) is a simple way of "getting rid of one's single status" (脱离光棍 **tuōlí guānggùn**).

我不怕过光棍节，怕的是我喜欢的人不过光棍节。
**wǒ bú pà guò guānggùnjié, pà de shì
wǒ xǐhuān de rén bú guò guānggùnjié.**
I am not afraid of Singles Day, I fear that
the person I like does not celebrate it.

## Last resting place

After "affordable housing" and the "affordable man," the Chinese are now looking for the "affordable grave" (经济适用坟 **jīngjì shìyòng fén**), a play on words that mocks the exorbitant cost of graves.

## The Lady Gaga effect
Among pop idols, Lady Gaga's Chinese name really stands out:

| 雷得嘎嘎 **léi de gāgā** Lady Gaga | Lightning/thunder (the thunder that paralyzes you) |
|---|---|

The English expression "Oh my God" has been replaced by "Oh my Lady Gaga," which has even found its way into mainstream TV shows.

## German lesson
"There's an interesting word in German."

"Really, what's that?"

"Tschüss. It means 'goodbye.' It also has a pronunciation close to the Chinese (去死 **qù sǐ**), which means 'Go to hell!'"

"There's another one, too."

"Really? What's that?"

"**Schade,** which means 'it is a pity' in German and 'stupid' in Chinese (傻的 **shǎ de**)."

## Japanese lesson

The same characters are used in several different languages but can have quite different meanings and provoke misunderstandings. Let's compare Chinese and Japanese.

Here are three well-known examples:

| Characters | Meaning and pronunciation in Chinese | Meaning and pronunciation in Japanese |
|---|---|---|
| 大丈夫 | **dàzhàngfu** <br> A true man/a loyal man | **daijōbu** <br> No problem! |
| 切手 | **qiēshǒu** <br> To cut one's hand | **kitte** <br> A stamp |
| 勉强 | **miǎnqiáng** <br> Push oneself hard/ to be reluctant | **benkyō** <br> To study |

# Magic Numbers, for Texting Addicts and Internet Users

Thanks to abundant homophones and near homophones, as well as popular usage, numbers have become very useful for texting addicts and Internet users alike. If you read the numbers out loud you get an idea of the meaning. Below are three messages. Please be aware that in the texting language, "you" (你 **nǐ**) is either translated by "1" or "0."

## An invitation

| Number | Decoding | Full sentence |
|--------|----------|---------------|
| 917753<br>**jiǔ yī qī qī wǔ sān** | 叫你去吃午餐<br>**jiào nǐ qù chī wǔ cān** | I am contacting you to have lunch together |
| 5366<br>**wǔ sān liù liù** | 我想聊聊<br>**wǒ xiǎng liáoliáo** | I would like to chat |
| 729<br>**qī èr jiǔ** | 去喝酒!<br>**qù hējiǔ!** | Let's go and have a drink! |
| 246<br>**èr sì liù** | 饿死了!<br>**è sǐ le!** | I am starving! |
| 5791<br>**wǔ qī jiǔ yī** | 我去找你<br>**wǒ qù zhǎo nǐ** | I will pick you up |
| 4242<br>**sì èr sì èr** | 是啊是啊<br>**shì ā shì ā** | Fine |

## A romance

| Number | Decoding | Full sentence |
|--------|----------|---------------|
| 14517<br>**yī sì wǔ yī qī** | 你是我氧气<br>**nǐ shì wǒ yǎngqì** | You are my oxygen |
| 8151<br>**bā yī wǔ yī** | 抱你吻你<br>**bào nǐ wěn nǐ** | Take you in my arms and kiss you |
| 21475<br>**èr yī sì qī wǔ** | 爱你是幸福<br>**ài nǐ shì xìngfú** | To love you is happiness |
| 521<br>**wǔ èr yī** | 我爱你<br>**wǒ ài nǐ** | I love you |

125

## A relationship's breakup

| Number | Decoding | Full sentence |
|---|---|---|
| 5376<br>**wǔ sān qī liù** | 我生气了<br>**wǒ shēng qì le** | I'm angry |
| 18574<br>**yī bā wǔ qī sì** | 你把我气死<br>**nǐ bǎ wǒ qì sǐ** | You get on my nerves |
| 148561<br>**yī sì bā wǔ liù yī** | 你是白痴无药医<br>**nǐ shì báichī wú yàoyī** | You are a hopeless idiot |
| 898<br>**bā jiǔ bā** | 分手吧<br>**fēnshǒu bā** | Let's split up |
| 88<br>**bābā** | 拜拜<br>**bàibài** | Bye-bye |

## Why did more couples get married in 2013 and 2014?

"You" (你 **nǐ**) is either represented with "0" or "1." So "I love you" can be written as 521 or 520.

The years 2013 and 2014 are special for people wishing to get married.

| Numbers | Decoding | Full sentence |
|---------|----------|---------------|
| 2013<br>**èr líng yī sān** | 爱你一生<br>**ài nǐ yī shēng** | I love you for my whole life |
| 2014<br>**èr líng yī sì** | 爱你一世<br>**ài nǐ yī shì** | I love you forever |

> 在一起时，1314是一生一世。
> 分手后，1314是一生一死。
> **zài yīqǐ shí, 1314 shì yīshēngyīshì.**
> **Fēnshǒu hòu, 1314 shì yīshēngyīsǐ.**
> When together, 1314 means "for life." After breaking up, 1314 means "it's over for life."

## The secret numbers

Numbers can also be used as amusing adjectives:

| Numbers | Word or expression | Explanation |
|---------|--------------------|-------------|
| 2 | 二 **èr** | Fool |
| 38 | 三八 **sān bā** | Bad tongue |
| 250 | 二百五 **èr bǎi wǔ** | Idiot |
| 290 | 二九零 **èr jiǔ líng** | Mad |

A popular combination is 290 = 250 + 38 + 2. It means that a madman is an idiot who not only has a bad tongue, but is a fool as well!

# Online Catchphrases

Nowadays, the "Web insects" (网虫 **wǎngchóng**) have ousted the bookworms of yesterday and new expressions emerge daily from the Net. Here are a few cult ones:

| 很黄很暴力<br>**hěn huáng hěn bàolì** | Very erotic, very violent (also translated as very pornographic, very violent) |
|---|---|

A schoolgirl was reported in the media as saying this about a Web advertisement. This hilarious and incongruous quote was parodied on the Internet and became notorious.

Later on, it was deformed to "very foolish, very naïve" (很傻 很天真 **hěn shǎ hěn tiānzhēn**), with reference to the unhappy romantic affair of a Hong Kong star.

| 猪坚强 **zhūjiānqiáng** | The strong-willed pig |
|---|---|

A pig was found alive in the debris of the 2008 Sichuan earthquake, having survived for 36 days by drinking rain water. People were touched by the animal's tenacity and the saying arose to describe a show of courage in a difficult situation.

| 打酱油 **dǎ jiàngyóu** | I'm going to buy soy sauce |
|---|---|

A journalist interviewing a passer-by one day was told "I'm going to buy soy sauce" and the sentence instantly became synonymous with "It's none of my business." The speaker wanted to avoid giving his opinion on a complicated question.

| 人生就像茶几，上面摆满了杯具。<br>**rénshēng jiù xiàng chájī, shàng-miàn bǎimǎnle bēijù.** | Life is like a tea table, with bitter cups placed all over it. |

This is a play on the homophones for "tragedy" (悲剧 **bēijù**) and "cup" (杯具 **bēijù**).

| 嫁人就嫁灰太狼，做人要做懒羊羊。<br>**jiàrén jiù jià huī tàiláng, zuòrén yào zuò lǎn yángyáng.** | Better to marry the big gray wolf and live like the lazy sheep. |

This catch phrase derives from a popular cartoon entitled *Pleasant Goat and Big Big Wolf,* which takes place in a world of geek sheep. The Lazy Sheep character in the series personifies intelligence and kindness, since he always rescues the other sheep when the Gray Wolf tries to catch them. By contrast, the wolf is incapable of bringing back prey, and his wife knocks him out with a frying pan and mocks him.

The Gray Wolf may look sinister, yet he now embodies the perfect husband. He is always willing, diligent, and considerate towards his wife. He cooks and spends freely to make her happy.

| 你信不信，反正我信了。<br>**nǐ xìn bú xìn, fǎnzhèng wǒ xìn le.** | Whether or not you believe this, I believe it. |

After the 2011 Wenzhou train crash, a senior official spoke these words when attempting to explain the inadequate rescue efforts. The quote was picked up instantly.

| 羡慕嫉妒恨！<br>**xiànmù jídù hèn!** | Jealousy, envy, and hatred! |

This three words are used together when congratulating somebody and indicating that you wish the same for yourself.

| Hold 住 **HOzhù** | Keep cool!/Hold it! |

The Taiwanese actress Miss Lin was all the rage on the Web when she used this funny word in a comedy show. She appeared to have studied fashion in Paris and therefore speak Mandarin with a French touch. It has now spread widely, but the meaning can evolve, depending on the situation. The "hold" part is pronounced "ho," without the "l" and the "d."

| 你幸福吗? **nǐ xìngfú ma?** | Are you happy? |

At the end of 2012, when CCTV (Central China Television) interviewed a passer-by, he misunderstood the question and replied: "My family name is not FU, it is ZENG." The fact is, this question sounds like "Is your family name FU?" (你姓福吗 **nǐ xìng fú ma?**)

| 我能说真话吗? **wǒ néng shuō zhēn huà ma?** | Can I say bad words? |

This was a driver's disgruntled answer to a journalist's question about the rise in gasoline prices at the pump.

| 你摊上大事了! **nǐ tānshàng dàshì le!** | You have got into big trouble! |

This became a catchphrase during Chinese New Year in 2013 on the occasion of a talk show.

| 法海你不懂爱! **Fǎhǎi nǐ bù dǒng ài!** | Fahai, you do not know anything about love! |

This stems from a popular song from early 2013. Fahai is a character from the *Legend of the White Snake*. The story goes that he does his best to prevent the two main characters from loving each other.

# English Loanwords: Mixing Languages

When foreign words come into the Chinese language, the results can take a poetic turn:

| Miniskirt | 迷你裙 **mí nǐ qún** | The skirt that turns your head |
|---|---|---|
| Playboy | 花花公子 **huāhuā gōngzǐ** | A prince surrounded by flowers |

花花公子
**huāhuā gōngzǐ**
A prince surrounded by flowers

Foreign abbreviations and acronyms may also acquire interesting meanings:

| BMW | 别摸我！ **Bié Mō Wǒ!** | Do not touch me! |
|---|---|---|
| IQ | 爱 **ài Q** | Love quotient |
| MSN | 摸死你 **Mō Sǐ Nǐ** | I am dying to touch/caress you |
| H&M | 后妈 **Hòu Mā** | Stepmother |

## The mixing of languages and pronunciation

### ■ English pronunciation

To learn the language of Shakespeare, you only need a pinch of imagination to play with the pronunciation.

| English | Chinese pronunciation | Meaning |
|---------|----------------------|---------|
| Agony | 爱过你 **ài guò nǐ** | I loved you |
| Animal | 爱你猫 **ài nǐ māo** | Love your cat! |
| Ambition | 俺必胜 **ǎn bì shèng** | I must win (俺 **ǎn** is a colloquial word for "I") |
| Ambulance | 俺不能死 **ǎn bù néng sǐ** | I do not wish to die |
| Economy | 依靠农民 **yīkào nóngmín** | To depend on farmers |
| To fly | 福来 **fú lái** | Happiness has arrived |
| Judge | 榨汁 **zhà zhī** | To extract juice |
| Thank you | 三克油 **sān kè yóu** | Three grams of oil |
| Taxi | 太可惜（了）**tài kěxī (le)** | What a pity! |
| Young | 羊 **yáng** | A sheep or goat |

Just like "I love tiger oil" (爱老虎油 **ài lǎohǔ yóu**), the phonetic translation of "I love you" has become very famous due to a popular Chinese movie. Another cult phrase among students learning English is "How old are you?" which translates word for word as 怎么老是你 **zěnme lǎo shì nǐ**, and is used to make fun of people with no aptitude for foreign language learning.

| English | Chinese pronunciation | Meaning |
|---------|----------------------|---------|
| Facebook | 非死不可 **fēi sǐ bùkě** | You have to die one day |
| iPad | 爱怕的 **ài pà de** | To fear heartbreak |
| iPhone | 爱疯 **àifēng** | To love like crazy |

爱疯!
**àifēng!**
iPhone!
Love like crazy!

## ■ Pronunciation games

Originally the Chinese use 首席财务官 **shǒuxí cáiwù guān** to say "Chief Financial Officer," but they also use the American direct translation.

| 公司负财官 | 公司腐败官 |
|-----------|-----------|
| **gōngsī fùcái guān** | **gōngsī fǔbài guān** |
| Chief Financial Officer | the corrupt company officer |

Mixing foreign and Chinese words can produce weird linguistic mutations:

| Bikini | 比基尼考 **bǐjīní kǎo** |
|--------|------------------------|
| | **Bikinikao** is used for students who are not in a hurry to study for their "exams" (考 **kǎo**) |

## ■ Fashion warning!

It is trendy in China to wear T-shirts with Western language words written on them, while the use of Chinese characters is spreading itself in Europe and the United States, especially for tattoos. The result is sometimes baffling, such as the characters 棺材 **guāncái**, meaning "coffin" as a Tattoo, which the wearer presumably did not understand! Similarly, T-shirts in China often have surprising Western words on them, which has triggered considerable debate. It has become common practice among parents to check what's written on their offspring's clothing with the help of a dictionary.

## ■ When counterfeit brands become brand names

The word "Shanzhai" (山寨 **shānzhài**) stands for "mountain stronghold" or "village of robbers." Today, it is used for counterfeit brands that have become brands in their own right — in other words, when a famous logo is imitated and applied to cheaper, lesser quality but widely available products. Young people particularly crave these goods. It all started with a highly successful 山寨 **shānzhài** brand cell phone, before spreading to numerous other sectors, such as computing, fashion, advertising, and even TV programs.

Examples of Shanzhai include Nokia, which has been changed to Nokla; others include KFC to KFG; Gucci to Cucci; Adidas to Adidos; Kappa to Kaobao; Toshiba to Tochifa; iPhone to Hiphone; and Sony to Sqny and Tony. These new brands have become a social phenomenon: critics argue they are forgeries that stifle all creativity, while supporters consider it fun and a way of thumbing their noses at the elite, expensive brands. Fake brands occur not only in China, but worldwide.

# Some Buzzwords in 2013 and 2014

## ■ Too tired to love

| | |
|---|---|
| 我再也不相信爱情了。<br>**wǒ zài yě bù xiāngxìn àiqíng le.** | I'll never believe in love again. |

## ■ Can a human being do this?

> 经理说了，今年所有人都不加工资。
> **jīnglǐ shuō le, jīnnián suǒyǒu rén dōu bù jiā gōngzī.**
> The manager said he will not increase the wages
> of any of us this year.

> 这是人干事吗?
> **zhe shì rén gàn shì ma?**
> Can a human being do this?

| 人干事！**rén gàn shì !** |
|---|
| These 3 Chinese characters are the abbreviation of the question: Has this been done by a human being ? |
| 这是**人干**的**事**吗? **zhè shì RÉN GÀN de SHÌ ma?** |

## ■ too young, too simple 图样图森破 tú yàng tú sēn pò

> 如果你不讨价还价，就是图样图森破。
> **rúguǒ nǐ bù tǎojiàhuánjià,**
> **jiù shì tú yàng tú sēn pò.**
> If you do not bargain a price,
> you are too young too simple.

■ **Please allow me to make a sad expression**

| 请允悲 qǐng yǔn bēi |
|---|
| These 3 Chinese characters are the abbreviation of the sentence: "Please allow me to make a sad expression." |
| **请允**许我做一个**悲**伤的表情。<br>**QǏNG YǓN**xǔ wǒ zuò yī gè **BĒI**shāng de biǎoqíng. |

地球是运动的，一个人不会
永远处在倒霉的位置。
dì qiú shì yùndòng de, yī gè rén bú huì
yǒngyuǎn chǔ zài dǎoméi de wèizhì.
Earth is in motion, a person cannot
always be in a bad position.

请允悲！
qǐng yǔn bēi!
Please allow me to make a sad expression!

■ **Life is so hard, some things do not need to be revealed**

| 人艰不拆 rén jiān bù chāi |
|---|
| These 4 Chinese characters are the abbreviation of the sentence: "Life is so hard, some things do not need to be revealed." |
| **人**生已经如此的**艰**难，有些事情就**不**要**拆**穿。<br>**RÉN**shēng yǐjīng rúcǐ de **JIĀN**nán,<br>yǒu xiē shìqíng jiù **BÚ** yào **CHĀI**chuān. |

| 不明觉厉 bù míng jué lì |
| --- |
| This phrase is composed of 4 Chinese characters. It is the abbreviation of the sentence: "although I do not understand what he/she says, it sounds brilliant." |
| 虽然**不明**白她说什么，但**觉**得很**厉**害。<br>**suīrán BÙ MÍNGbái tā shuō shénme, dàn JUÉdé hěn LÌhài.** |

## ■ There is no cure

| 何弃疗 hé qì liáo |
| --- |
| These 3 Chinese characters are the abbreviation of the sentence: "Why do you have to abandon the cure?" |
| 为**何**要放**弃**治**疗**？ **wéi HÉ yào fàngQÌ zhìLIÁO?** |

## ■ To be class (open-minded with a fine taste)
高端大气上档次 gāoduān dàqì shàngdàngcì

This phrase can also be used in a derogative way.

> 你会说法语，你很高端大气上档次！
> **nǐ huì shuō fǎyǔ, nǐ hěn gāoduān dàqì shàngdàngcì!**
> You can speak French, you are so class!

## ■ A nice personality will bring success in the end
人品大爆发 rénpǐn dà bàofā

> 你居然考试过了，你真是人品大爆发！
> **nǐ jūrán kǎoshì guò le, nǐ zhēn shì rénpǐn dà bàofā !**
> You passed your exams, your nice personality
> has been rewarded!

## ■ Demonstrate the limit of your IQ 秀下限 xiù xiàxiàn

137

## Some Interesting Stories and a Taste of Chinese Humor

For the New Year, it is a tradition in China to put couplets on the doors. Internet users sometimes create funny ones.

| | |
|---|---|
| 我是单身。**wǒ shì dānshēn.** | I am single. |
| 去年光棍，今年光棍，明年好像还是光棍。<br>**qù nián guānggùn, jīn nián guānggùn, míng nián hǎo xiàng hái shì guānggùn.** | I was single last year, single this year and apparently I will still be single next year. |
| 同事有主，同学有主，同龄似乎全都有主。<br>**tóngshì yǒu zhǔ, tóngxué yǒu zhǔ, tónglíng sìhū quán dōu yǒu zhǔ.** | My colleagues have a friend, my classmates have a friend, people of my age seem to be all taken. |

单身并不难，难的是应付那些千方百计想让你结束单身的人。
**dānshēn bìng bù nán, nán de shì yīngfù nà xiē qiān fāng bǎi jì xiǎng ràng nǐ jiéshù dānshēn de rén.**
To be single is not difficult. The difficulty is with the others, who think about every possible way to end your single life.

138

## In search of a soulmate

Search ads for a soulmate (征婚 **zhēnghūn**) are common on the net. Here are 3 diverted examples:

Man, 28 years old, 1.60m

According to tradition, "ignorance is the virtue of women." Today, the world has largely evolved. Women have entered the labor market and are considered half of the sky. My future wife should have a good academic background, but not better than mine, and it should be the same for her income. Should it not be the case, she will have to demonstrate pragmatism and show a sense of balance.

Man, 38 years old, 1.70m

I did brilliantly in primary school, and now I am contemplating studying in a large university. Currently, I work in a multinational company as a white collar (sweeper at Kentucky Fried Chicken). My salary is 800 yuan (about US$128), I have a means of transportation (a bike) and I live in a flat in joint tenancy (a dorm). I want to meet a beautiful 25-year-old young woman, courageous and hardworking, to spend together some happy days.

Female, 40 years old, 1.65m

Recently divorced, I look younger than my actual age and look about 30. I am a gourmet cook for someone who has never had a health problem. I will take care of the gentleman who is to be my husband. If you are a nice person with a cast iron stomach, write to me!

我的优点是我很帅，但是我的缺点是我帅的不明显！
**wǒ de yōudiǎn shì wǒ hěn shuài,
dànshì wǒ de quēdiǎn shì wǒ shuài de bú míngxiǎn!**
My advantage is that I am handsome,
but my disadvantage is I am handsome but not understood!

## To Be Or Not To Be

2b or not 2b that is the question...

2b means "to be stupid" in Chinese Internet language.

## Destiny

| 男人要有钱，<br>**nánrén yào yǒu qián,** | If a man has money, |
|---|---|
| 和谁都有缘。<br>**hé shéi dōu yǒu yuán.** | he will find his destiny with anyone. |

## What does it take to be a man?

| 一生儿女债，半世老婆奴。<br>**yī shēng ér nǚ zhài, bànshì lǎopó nú.** | We have debts our whole life for our children, and for half of our life we are the slaves of our spouse. |
|---|---|

## "All you need is love"

| | |
|---|---|
| 单身是山路。<br>**dānshēn shì shānlù.** | Being a bachelor is a mountain road. |
| 恋爱是大路。<br>**liàn'ài shì dàlù.** | Love is an avenue. |
| 分手是岔路。<br>**fēnshǒu shì chàlù.** | A breakup is a crossroad. |
| 试婚是探路。<br>**shìhūn shì tànlù.** | Living together before being married is like exploring a road. |
| 结婚是绝路。<br>**jiéhūn shì juélù** | Getting married is an impasse. |
| 重婚是短路。<br>**chónghūn shì duǎnlù.** | Bigamy is a short circuit. |
| 离婚是活路。<br>**líhūn shì huólù.** | Divorce is a feasible method. |
| 再婚是死路。<br>**zàihūn shì sǐlù.** | Remarriage is a dead end. |

## A Chinese Adam and Eve?

"If Adam and Eve had been Chinese the world would have been different."

"Why do you think so?"

"Well, they would have eaten the worm, not the apple!"

## Gleaned from the Chinese website of a specialist French travel agency

"The 20-year-old woman may be compared to a rugby ball: a crowd of men run after the ball.

"The 30-year-old woman may be compared to a basketball: a few men run after the ball.

"The 40-year-old woman may be compared to a ping-pong ball: the ball is thrown by one man and returned by another.

"The 50-year-old woman may be compared to a golf ball: the further it is sent off, the better."

*From *Voyage Interculturels France-Chine*

## Popular perceptions

At the age of 20 a man wants to marry a woman of 20.
At the age of 30 a man wishes to marry a woman of 20.
At the age of 40 a man aspires to marry a woman of 20.
At the age of 50 a man dreams of marrying a woman of 20.

Popular wisdom wants it that a woman is comparable to a cucumber or a tofu until the age of 30.

## Extract from *The Good Women of China: Hidden Voices* by Xinran

"Glasses in hand, men often start talking about women. Love would be comparable to a 'swordfish' with good taste but full of bones. The personal secretaries would inevitably be thought of as 'carps': the more they simmer, the better they will be. Wives of other men are like 'Japanese *fugu*' — one bite can kill, but risking death is a source of pride. Their own wives are comparable to 'salted cod,' because they keep longer in salt. They are best when there is nothing else, and cod remains economical. They make a main dish with rice."

## Implacable logic

Some people claim that love is like a heart tied to a kite. Everyone talks about it but only a very few are lucky enough to catch it.

## Male friendship

A wife says to her husband, "Do you know what your best friend would say if I called him to ask him where you were?"

"No," replied the husband.

So the wife called his best friend and asked him, "Is my husband with you?"

The best friend replied, "Yes, he was with me, but he has just left."

The wife put the phone down. A few seconds later her husband's cell phone rang. It was his best friend calling. "Hurry up, your wife is looking for you," he said.

The wife turned to her husband and said, "Now you know."

## A touch of philosophy

At the age of 20 we are ready to fight and sacrifice ourselves for high ideals; but with age we are merely content with what we have.

## A riddle

"Guess who often calls you and always wants you to be there in emergencies, but totally ignores you when you are in need?"

"My mistress?"

"No."

"My wife?"

"No, your bank."

## Three categories of men

When women dream of marriage they think of a prince charming on a white horse. The horse has come to symbolize the perfect man, but unfortunately perfect men are few and far between. In the happiness market there are more monkeys, or second-rate men. If you miss the opportunity to find a monkey then you'll have to make do with a mule, which symbolizes the last category.

## How to pick up a husband

An ordinary man who had the audacity to ask a celebrity for her hand in marriage, was told: "I would rather cry in a Mercedes than laugh on the back of your bicycle." Later on, the celebrity had to excuse herself publicly.

## In court

This scene takes place in a court in southern China. When the defense lawyer arrived, he started shouting at the prosecutor, "You swindler, you cheat people!"

"You are a downright liar," the other replied.

The judge solemnly tapped his gavel: "Now that the introductions have been made, the hearing is open."

## Sweet heart

When they are single, women are like doves. In love, they follow the unbearable lightness of their hearts in search of their dream.

When they become engaged they are more like swallows. While their heart still has wings, it only rarely tries them out.

After 20 years of marriage, they resemble ducks. They would like to fly to other places, but they cannot.

## A Chinese challenge

During a press conference one day, Yang Jiechi, a senior Chinese politician, said: "Chinese is one of the easiest languages to learn, otherwise it would be hard to explain why 1.3 billion people choose Chinese as their mother tongue."

## The boss and the employee

The boss told an employee he had just fired, "I understand that you want to go to the cemetery after I die to spit on my grave?"

"Do not worry," replied the man he recently fired, "I have changed my mind, I will not have the patience to stand in line!"

## A dog's life

On summer's day, should you come face-to-face with a crazy Doberman dog, do not be afraid, just be brave and face it. All in all, there are three possible outcomes:

The first is that you win the battle, and you are better than a dog.

The second is that you are quits and you are worth no more than a dog.

The third is that you lose and you are worth less than a dog.

## The car buyer

A peasant went into town to buy a car. He saw a Santana 2000 in the window and called out to the car salesman.

"This car is for 2,000 RMB, I'll buy it!" (about US$325)

"That's not the price, that's the model," replied the salesman. But the buyer wasn't having any of it. "Just look across the road," he insisted, "There's a Mercedes 600."

## A domestic journey

In Beijing, you feel like a provincial.
In Dongbei, you become brave.
In Shenzhen, everyone is busy.
In Chengdu, life is sweeter.
In Hainan, people take their time.
In Shanghai, you polish your style.
In Wenzhou, you learn real business.
In Tianjin, you cultivate your sense of humor.

## Two worlds, two viewpoints

A man is his wife's entire world, whereas a wife is only half of a man's world.

## The ideal husband

In Shanghai, men are good cooks.
In Beijing, they like politics.
In Dongbei, they are sure of themselves.

## The "Three Submissions and the Four Virtues"

In ancient China a woman was expected to submit to her father, then to her husband, and if widowed, to her son. She also had to respect the virtues of morality, proper speech, modesty, and diligence. Today, out of humor, these virtues have been changed to apply to men as follows:

If a man's wife wants to go and have fun, he must accompany her.

Her orders must be executed.

If in doubt, he must obey without discussion.

When she's getting ready to go out, he must never show impatience.

On her birthday, he must never forget to buy presents.

When buying them he must spend generously.

In the event of a quarrel, he must accept everything.

## A successful marriage

If a stupid man marries a stupid woman, the marriage will be a success.

If a stupid man marries an intelligent woman, the marriage will end in divorce.

If an intelligent man marries a stupid woman, he will have a "private secretary" (a mistress).

If an intelligent man marries an intelligent woman, their romance will flourish.

## The "Three Perfections"

Previously the "Three Perfections" (三好 **sān hǎo**) referred to a student who was diligent in ethics, studied hard, and had good health. Today, for the fun of it, people

say what actually matter is success in exams, beauty, and parents' connections.

## A couple's life

Everybody knows that the relationship between spouses may evolve after marriage. If we untangle an expression meaning "to be overjoyed" (喜出望外 **xǐchū wàngwài**), what happens to all couples becomes crystal clear: "happiness leaves" (喜出 **xǐ chū**) and "hope goes out the window" (望外 **wàngwài**).

## The practitioner

When a "doctor" (医生 **yīshēng**) behaves like a "business-man" (商人 **shāngrén**), he is called a "business-loving doctor" (医商 **yī shāng**).

## Audi or Dior?

Sometimes switching the characters around leads to a few surprises. One example is "Audi" (奥迪 **àodí**), which produces "Dior" (迪奥 **dí'ào**)!

## Genius or talent?

Only two strokes mark the difference between "genius" (天才 **tiāncái**) and "talent" (人才 **réncái**). Which one are you?

## The fashionista

Who would have doubted it? The fashionista may "at first sight" (一见 **yíjiàn**) "fall in love" (钟情 **zhōngqíng**). But by changing one character you have her "fall in love with the first item of clothing she sees" (衣见钟情 **yī jiàn zhōngqíng**).

## Expert or charlatan?

"Experts" (专家 **zhuānjiā**) may not be all that they claim to be. If they turn out to be incompetent, they are frauds and are called "charlatans" (砖家 **zhuānjiā**), a pun created just for them.

## The real thing

Woman: "I no longer believe in love at first sight."
Her friend: "Oh, why is that?"
Woman: "How can you tell how much a man earns at first sight?"

## Wisdom

"It is not the road that is not straight, it is you who cannot walk."

## A cute mouse

If you look closely, the "at" sign (@) looks much like a "little mouse" (小老鼠 **xiǎo lǎoshǔ**).

## Twisted words

| A partner/associate<br>伙伴 **huǒbàn** | An enthusiastic partner<br>火伴 **huǒbàn** |
|---|---|
| A fellow student<br>同学 **tóngxué** | A friend who wears the same shoes<br>同鞋 **tóngxié** (another popular interpretation is "children's shoes," 童鞋 **tóngxié**) |
| Stress<br>压力 **yālì** | A Beijing pear<br>鸭梨 **yālí** |

## Politics

It's no surprise that "politics" (政治 **zhèngzhì**) sounds like "to quarrel" (争执 **zhēngzhí**).

## A man's life

At the age of 20 a man is an unfinished product; at 40 he is a quality product; at 50 he is a superior product; and at 70 he ends up as a decorative item.

## Filial piety

To fear your father is proof of filial piety.
To fear your wife is to show affection.

## Environmental awareness

Two things pollute people's lives: waste pollutes their environment, and money pollutes their thoughts.

## Misunderstanding

A tourist in Beijing hailed a passer-by, but instead of responding she scurried past him. It turns out that the tourist had said, "May I kiss you?" (亲吻 **qīn wěn**) instead of "May I ask you...?" (请问 **qǐng wèn**).

# Mao Zedong's Works and Modern Couples

Netizens cleverly compare Mao Zedong's works and marital relationships.

1. To fall in love would be to "Combat Liberalism" (a text written by Mao in 1937). In this case, liberaism is understood as egoism.

2. One's first love may be considered "On Practice" (1937).

3. Quarrels between spouses relate to "On Contradiction" (1937).

4. When the quarrels are never-ending, they become "On Protracted War" (1938).

5. Having a child is "Our Economic Policy" (1934).

6. When a husband takes a mistress, it could be called "On Coalition Government" (1945); but for the wife it means "Problems of Strategy in Guerilla War Against Japan" (1938).

7. If the husband changes his mind, the wife will view the situation as "On the War Criminals Suing for Peace" (1949), but she will also "Cast Away Illusions, Prepare for Struggle" (1949). If they don't end up divorcing, the situation may be to "Carry the Revolution Through to the End" (1948).

8. In the case of a re-marriage, the couple can "Greet the New High Tide of the Chinese Revolution" (1947).

## Marriage and Divorce

Marriage is like looking in the same direction together (比); divorce is like standing back to back (北).

## Laozi and Confucius

孔子不能解决的问题，
老子帮你解决。
**Kǒngzǐ bù néng jiějué de wèntí,
Lǎozǐ bāng nǐ jiějué.**
If Confucius cannot solve your
problem, Laozi can do it.

Explanation: In Chinese language, Laozi has two meanings—it refers to Laozi, the father of Taoism, but it can also mean "me" or "I."

## Chinese brain-teasers

How to interpret freely the Chinese word for "happiness" (幸福 **xìngfú**)?

By deciphering the characters that make up the word "happiness," this term conveys a simple message: "To be wealthy enough to have a roof over one's and one's family's head, nice clothes, and enough to eat."

幸 **xìng** is made up of two parts:

- 土 **tǔ** (above), meaning "earth" (taken here as property)
- ¥ **Yi** (below) is an old character used in ancient China and symbolizes money

福 **fú** is made up of four parts:

- 衤 **yī** (on the left side) means "clothing"
- 一 (on the right side and above) represents a roof
- 口 **kǒu** (on the right side in the middle) means "the mouth" and symbolizes here the members of the family
- 田 **tián** (on the right side below) means "fields" and symbolizes wealth

## Chen Shimei and Pan Jinlian

| Chinese | translation |
|---|---|
| 女人最恨的男人是陈世美；男人最喜欢的女人是潘金莲。 **nǚrén zuì hèn de nánrén shì Chén Shìměi; nánrén zuì xǐhuān de nǚrén shì Pān Jīnlián.** | Women avoid the type of men that resemble Chen Shimei; men like the type of women that resemble Pan Jinlian. |
| In Beijing opera, Chen Shimei is a character who leaves his wife for another love. In a famous novel, Pan Jinlian is married and has a lover. | |

## The crisis

The Chinese word for crisis is 危机 **wēijī**. The first character "危 **wēi**" means "danger," while the second "机 **jī**" means "opportunity." Make no mistake, there is a long road to go between the two.

## White-collar workers

The White Demon is a figure from the great Chinese classic, *Journey to the West*. Today, it refers to white-collar workers. It is easy to understand why, when we analyze the three characters it is composed of:

| Expression | White Demon 白骨精 báigǔjīng | | |
|---|---|---|---|
| Explanation | white collar 白领 báilǐng | competent 骨干 gǔgàn | elite 精英 jīngyīng |

## Modern evolution

古代有权就有钱，现代有钱就有权。

**gǔdài yǒu quán jiù yǒu qián, xiàndài yǒu qián jiù yǒu quán.**

In ancient times, if you had power, you had money. Nowadays, if you have money, you have power.

## Wisdom

爱情是享受，婚姻是忍受。

**àiqíng shì xiǎngshòu, hūnyīn shì rěnshòu.**

Love is to enjoy, marriage is to endure.

## Practice

恋爱需要实习，分手需要练习。

**liàn'ài xūyào shíxí, fēnshǒu xūyào liànxí.**

Falling in love requires practice, breaking up requires training.

## Popular saying

仁者见仁，智者见智，愚者见愚。

**rénzhě jiàn rén, zhìzhě jiàn zhì, yúzhě jiàn yú.**

The benevolent man sees benevolence, the wise man sees wisdom, the fool sees stupidity (in other words, everyone has their own point of view).

## Speech fine-tuning

该说的说，不该说的小声说。

**gāi shuō de shuō, bù gāi shuō de xiǎo shēng shuō.**

Say what absolutely has to be said, and say in a low voice what should not be absolutely said.

# Postscript

Eminently creative, the Middle Kingdom has always been able to reinvent itself by adapting to foreign influences. That specific Chinese know-how has centuries-old roots.

To be continued...

## Websites

www.baike.baidu.com
http://blog.sina.com.cn
www.china.org.cn
www.chinadaily.com.cn
http://chine.aujourdhuilemonde.com
www.chine-informations.com
www.chine-nouvelle.com
www.chinesecio.cn
http://chineseculture.about.com
http://gb.cri.cn
http://cultural-china.com
www.globaltimes.cn
www.haha365.com
www.ifeng.com
www.ishuo.cn
www.nciku.com
www.qq.com/
www.sina.com.cn
www.sohu.com
www.theworldofchinese.com
www.tianya.cn
www.wenming.cn
http://wenwen.soso.com
http://www.wikipedia.org
www.xiaohuayoumo.com
www.xinhuanet.com
http://www.wllxy.net/

http://chengyu.911cha.com/
http://yulu.so/
http://yulu.dxju.com/
http://www.dictall.com/
http://blog.voc.com.cn/
http://tieba.baidu.com/
www.kaixin001.com/
www.28hudong.com/
blog.sina.com.cn
http://www.202030.com/
http://www.duwenzhang.com/
zhidao.baidu.com
blog.renren.com
iask.sina.com.cn
tieba.baidu.com
www.china.com.cn/culture/
www.douban.com/
bbs.tianya.cn
zh.wikipedia.org/zh
i.youku.com
weibo.com
http://www.urbandictionary.com/
http://www.uni.edu/becker/chinese2.html
http://www.saporedicina.com/english/learn-chinese-online-25-excellent-free-resources/

## References

Fu Xingling, Chen Zhanghuan, Eds., *Changyong Gouci Zidian* (Dictionary of Common Words), Renmin University Press, PRC, 1984.

Guo Yuling, Dian Suwen, Xi Yongqin (Translator), "Speaking Chinese: 1,000 Practical Chinese Idioms," New World Press, China, 2002.

Hou Min, Zhou Jian, *2007 Hanyu Xinciyu* (New Words in 2007), Commercial Press, Beijing, 2008.

———, *2008 Hanyu Xinciyu* (New Words in 2008), Commercial Press, Beijing, 2009.

———, *2009 Hanyu Xinciyu* (New Words in 2009), Commercial Press, Beijing, 2010.

Kaku Meiki, Isobe Yuko, Taniuchi Mieko, "1,500 Japanese and Chinese Homophones," International University Foreign Language Press, Japan, 2011.

Li Han, "Shouji Humor, New Words from the Cool People's Tribe," China Civil Aviation Press, PRC, 2009.

Li Ke, "A Story of Lala's Promotion," Shaanxi Teacher's Training College, PRC, 2008.

Peng Peng, "Etiquette and Culture," Tsinghua University Press, PRC, 2007.

Wu Shuping, *Zhongguo Dansheng Nuxing Diaocha* (A Survey of Single Chinese Women), Xinhua Press, PRC, 2010.

Xu Zongcai, Ying Junling, *Suyu Cidian* (Dictionary of Popular Sayings), Commercial Press, PRC, 2006.

Yin Binyong, ed., "1,000 Common Chinese Idioms And Set Phrases," Beijing Teaching Press, PRC, 2001.

— — —, "100 Pearls Of Chinese Wisdom," Beijing Teaching Press, PRC, 2001.

— — —, "100 Chinese Two-Part Allegorical Sayings," Beijing Teaching Press, PRC, 2003.

Yu Jialou, "A Dictionary Of Chinese Idioms with English Translations," China Science and Technology University Press, 1998.

Zhang Jiehai, *Zhongguo Nanren Diaocha* (A Survey of Chinese Men), Jiangsu Art and Literature Press, 2009.

Zhou Lingzhong, "The Stories Behind 100 Chinese Idioms," Beijing Teaching Press, 2001.

## Photo Credits

The photos used in this book are sourced from the following websites:

123rf.com

Bigstockphoto.com

Canstockphoto.com

Dreamstime.com

Shutterstock.com

# Acknowledgments

I would like to thank the following people for their suggestions and encouragement:
Professor Tianfang Lei, Christian Hakim, Huang Wenhui, Qi Weihua, Yang Chen,
Zhang Wei, Zhong Na, Wang Jing, Firouzé Karimpour, Zhu Yu, Corinne and Richard Michel,
Nicholas Lachenby, Michaela Minty, Thierry Ragueneau, Professor Wang Peiwen,
the editor in Chief of Planète chinois Alain Labat, the translator Hervé Denès,
Passeport pour la Chine, Montargis China Friendship Association,
the Chinese language professors and Chinese cultural associations in France.

Published by Tuttle Publishing, an imprint of
Periplus Editions (HK) Ltd.

**www.tuttlepublishing.com**

Copyright © 2012 Editions Sepia
English edition © 2014 Periplus Editions (HK) Ltd
All rights reserved.

ISBN 978-0-8048-4463-9

Distributed by:

**North America, Latin America & Europe**
Tuttle Publishing
364 Innovation Drive,
North Clarendon VT 05759-9436, USA
Tel: 1 (802) 773 8930; Fax: 1 (802) 773 6993
info@tuttlepublishing.com
www.tuttlepublishing.com

**Japan**
Tuttle Publishing
Yaekari Building 3F 5-4-12 Osaki, Shinagawa-ku
Tokyo 141-0032, Japan
Tel: (81) 3 5437 0171; Fax: (81) 3 5437 0755
sales@tuttle.co.jp
www.tuttle.co.jp

**Asia Pacific**
Berkeley Books Pte. Ltd.
61 Tai Seng Avenue #02-12 Singapore 534167
Tel: (65) 6280-1330; Fax: (65) 6280-6290
inquiries@periplus.com.sg
www.periplus.com

18 17 16 15 14    5 4 3 2 1    1409HP
Printed in Singapore

TUTTLE PUBLISHING® is a registered trademark
of Tuttle Publishing, a division of
Periplus Editions (HK) Ltd.

### The Tuttle Story:
### "Books to Span the East and West"

Many people are surprised to learn that the world's largest publisher of books on Asia had its humble beginnings in the tiny American state of Vermont. The company's founder, Charles E. Tuttle, belonged to a New England family steeped in publishing.

Immediately after WW II, Tuttle served in Tokyo under General Douglas MacArthur and was tasked with reviving the Japanese publishing industry. He later founded the Charles E. Tuttle Publishing Company, which thrives today as one of the world's leading independent publishers.

Though a westerner, Tuttle was hugely instrumental in bringing a knowledge of Japan and Asia to a world hungry for information about the East. By the time of his death in 1993, Tuttle had published over 6,000 books on Asian culture, history and art—a legacy honored by the Japanese emperor with the "Order of the Sacred Treasure," the highest tribute Japan can bestow upon a non-Japanese.

With a backlist of 1,500 titles, Tuttle Publishing is more active today than at any time in its past—inspired by Charles Tuttle's core mission to publish fine books to span the East and West and provide a greater understanding of each.